Inside this book! *The Most Exciting Thing to Happen to the English Language Since the Caxton Press in 1476.*

Jim Lovell (luvəl) woz having diner at thə Wiet Hous, wen hiz frend, Ed White (wiet) burnd too deph. Aktueəly, it wozn't realy diner Lovell woz having, just finger sandwichəz, o'rinj jooc, and unmémərəbəl wien, laid out on linən-kuverd taebəlz in thə Green Room. Aktueəly tóo, Ed White didn't realy burn too deph. Thə fuemz klaimd him long bifor thə flaemz ever kəd hav. (page 11)

If English is your main and first-learned language, you will be pleased to see some safeguards to preserve its richness of sounds, as it becomes the international language of planet Earth with its users in the billions.

Thair woz noe spaes in thə tieny kabin for nervəs paesing. Ə skant aet feet sepəraetəd thə horlwae entrəns from thə smorl port'hoel, that shoed thə dul blak ov spaes; and əkros thə distəns, from thə lokd dor on wun siedworl, too that on thee uther, kəd hav been spand bie thə ɣung man'z armz. Oenly hiz iez wer free too roem, and thae wer tieərd from endləs repətíshən. (page 13)

Derivations and History of Words will continue to be included in good dictionaries, so don't think that 'no nonsense' spelling will obscure this. (page 17)

Giving the **'foot, put, would'** vowel sounds their own vowel, because a very few of them might have two syllables and be stressed, is outside the philosophy of Inglish Maed Simpəl. **To make a case against 200 years of contrary agreement, leave out the vowels of 'foot, put, would'.** So now we have **'ft, pt, wd'**, ignoring the silent 'l' (el) of 'could, should or would'. **If you did this correctly, we now have 'fət, pət, wəd', whether we use our vowel of default or not!** (page 14)

A Soundsabet is an Alphabet of Sounds that we use in the Inglish language. It is more than ABC, since it includes the consonant diphthongs like **ch, ng, sh** and the two **th** sounds (as **ph** and **th**); the many vowel sounds that come from **a, e, i, o, u;** the **y** as a consonant (written **ɣ**); the **y** as a vowel (written **y**); and the most common 'a' sound as the backwards upside down 'e' or schwa (written **ə**) to separate it from the 'a' of 'hat'. (page 2)

<u>Inside This Book!</u>

Most of the time you will write the same way with even widely different accents, because the same soundsabet letters will have a different sound to you. (page 8)

At age 9…. **On the London Underground, I listened to my father converse in English with someone I was sure was <u>not</u> speaking English. But this man was Scots, from Glasgow, Scotland and he <u>was</u> speaking English!** In British East Africa, as it was then, my hearing had been limited to only 4 or 5 English accents, versus the many very distinctively different accents in Britain and Ireland (about 15), along with another four or five in North America.

Many years later the tables were turned when I took my American wife for a holiday in Britain and Ireland. **We were having lunch in a Welsh pub, and she listened to me speaking English to a local, that she felt very sure was talking back to me in Welsh!** (the Celtic language of Wales) **Of course, we both spoke English in two very different accents:** his accent being Welsh, and mine from southern England, modified by 15 years in Canada and the USA. (page 15)

About the Author: See last page (25a).

INGLISH MAED SIMPƏL

*English Should Be Written As It Sounds
& Spoken As It Is Written!*

Chris Marquis

Balboa Press books may be ordered through booksellers or by contacting:

Balboa Press
A Division of Hay House
1663 Liberty Drive
Bloomington, IN 47403
www.balboapress.com
1 (877) 407-4847

ISBN: 978-1-9822-4130-8 (sc)
ISBN: 978-1-9822-4129-2 (e)

Print information available on the last page.

Balboa Press rev. date: 09/04/2020

BALBOA.PRESS
A DIVISION OF HAY HOUSE

INGLISH MAED SIMPƏL (IMS)

English Should Be Written As It Sounds & Spoken As It Is Written!

While several languages succeed in doing this to various degrees, including French and Spanish, the English language has several different ways of saying a single letter, and several different ways of writing a single sound. As a living, changing, expanding language, it is not surprising how this has come about, as we have taken words from other languages and incorporated them in our own. **Words can follow any one of several different rules, as to spelling and pronunciation, depending on their etymology (word history).**

But it is not necessary to keep it that way. Our language can keep its history and continue to expand and evolve into planet Earth's international language. At the same time, it can be written as it sounds, and spoken as it is written, according to simple, invariable rules, that will permit a virtually flawless ease of spelling and pronunciation.

It will sound exactly as it did before. We call it simply ....**Inglish Maed Simpəl.** This is a **'How To' Manual for Students and Publishers of IMS**, but once the switch is made, it will, of course, be of great interest to all who use the English language. The title, Inglish Maed Simpəl, and its comparatively radical spelling, tells a lot. Two precise purposes will tell more:

PURPOSE:

"To Simplify The Spelling Of The English Language"

"To Enable Anyone To Pronounce & Spell English Words Correctly"

INGLISH MAED SIMPƏL (IMS)

Inglish shəd bee Ritən az it Soundz and Spoekən az it is Ritən!

Wiel sevrəl langwijəz sukséed in doing this too vairiəs dəgreez, inklóoding French and Spanish, thee Inglish langwij haz sevrəl difrənt waez ov saeing ə singəl leter, and sevrəl wayz ov rieting ə singəl sound. Az ə living, chaenjing, expánding langwij, it iz not surpríezing how this haz kum əbout, az wee taek werdz from ənúther langwij and inkórpəraet them in our oen. **Werdz kan foloe eny wun ov sevrəl difrənt roolz, az too speling and prənunsiáeshən, dəpénding on thair etimóləjy (werd histəry).**

But it iz not nesisəry too keep it that wae. Our langwij kan keep itz histəry and contínue too ivolv into planit Erph'z intənáshənəl langwij. At thə same tiem, it kan bee ritən az it soundz, and spoekən az it iz ritən, əkórding too simpəl, inváiriəbəl roolz, that wil pəmít an eez ov speling, and ə florləs eez ov prənunsiáeshən.

It wil sound igzáktly az it did bifór. Wee korl it simply ….Inglish Maed Simpəl. This iz ə **'Hou Too' Manueəl for Stuedənts and Publisherz ov IMS**, but wuns thə swich iz maed, it wil, ov kors, bee ov graet intrəst too orl hoo uez thee Inglish langwij. Thə tietəl, Inglish Maed Simpəl, and itz kəmpá'rətivly radikəl speling, telz ə lot. Wun or toó prəsíes perpəsəz wil tel mor.

PERPƏS:

"Too Simplifie Thə Speling Ov Thee Inglish Langwij"

"Too Ináebəl Enywun Too Prənóuns And Spel Inglish Werdz Kəréktly"

So let us go straight into the SOUNDSABETS. **A Soundsabet is an Alphabet of Sounds that we use in the Inglish language.** It is more than ABC, since it includes the consonant diphthongs like **ch, ng, sh** and the two **th** sounds (as **ph** and **th**); the many vowel sounds that come from **a, e, i, o, u;** the **y** as a consonant (written ɣ); the **y** as a vowel (written **y**); and the most common 'a' sound as the backwards/upside down **e** or schwa (written ə) to separate it from the **a** of 'hat'. As used here, a diphthong is defined as an unsegmentable gliding speech sound, represented by two or more letters. You will see vowel diphthongs **ay** and **oy (bay/boy)** using the vowel '**y**' instead of the consonant 'ɣ', reserved for words like **ɣeer/ɣear, bieɣoo, ɣeloe** and **biɣónd**; in Numbers Simplified, a treat to come perhaps, you will see 'ɣ' again, around number eighty.

One more thing to mention before introducing the Soundsabets is the choice of Basic IMS (BI) and Advanced IMS (AI). You will quickly see the difference and might have a preference for one or the other. **Should AI only be used, the theory of BI still helps to understand and analyse the subject.** By now you will have found the first page repeated in BI when you turned the page, and now in AI. Use of IMS like this will continue. **Be sure to read it.**

That is just enough theory up front to allow you to study and understand the Soundsabets, presented next. Just be sure to read and pronounce each line and syllable, preferably out loud. Notes on these two charts will immediately follow. **Look up any word not fully understood** in a good dictionary, the notes above, the notes following, or in the Glossary as it becomes available. There will be a Soundsabet in BI, followed by one in AI. After that, there will be a return to English (front page) and IMS (back).

Soe let us goe straet intoo thə SOUNDZƏBETS. **Ə Soundzəbet iz an Alfəbet ov Soundz that wee uez in thee Inglish langwij.** It iz mor than ABC, sinc it inklóodz thə konsənənt difphongz like **ch, ng, sh** and thə toȯ **th** soundz (az **ph** and **th**); thə meny vowəl soundz that kum from **a, e, i, o, u**; thə **y** az ə konsənənt (ritən **ɏ**); thə **y** az ə vowəl (ritən **y**); and thə moest komən 'a' sound az thə bakwədz/upsied down **e** or shwar (ritən **ə**) too sepəraet it from thə **a** of 'hat'. Az uezd heer, a difphong iz dəfíend az an unsegméntəbəl glieding speech sound reprizéntəd bẏ toȯ or mor leterz. Ɏoo wil see vowəl difphongz **ay** and **oy** (**bay/boy**), uezing thə vowəl '**y**' instéd ov thə konsənənt '**ɏ**', rəzérvd for werdz like **ɏeer/ ɏear, bieɏoo, ɏeloe** and **biɏónd**; in Numberz Simplified, ə treat too kum perhápz, yoo may see **ɏ** əgen, əround number aety.

Wun mor phing too menshən bifor intrədúecing thə toȯ Soundzəbetz iz thə choic ov Baesik IMS (BI) and Adváncd/Advárncd IMS (AI). Ɏoo wil qikly see thə difrənc* and miet hav ə prefrənc* for wun or thee uther. **Shəd AI oenly bee uezd, thə pheeəry ov BI stil helps too understand and anəlýz thə subject.** Bẏ now ɏoo wil hav found thə first paej rəpéatəd in BI wen yoo turnd thə paej, and now in AI. Ues ov IMS liek this wil kəntínue. **Bee shor too read it!**

That iz just inuf pheeəry up frunt too əlow yoo too study and understánd thə Soundzəbets, prizéntəd next. Just bee shor* too read and prənóunc each lien and siləbəl, preferəbly out loud. (*Sum werdz hav ə choic ov how thae ar sed, soe aulsoe ə choic ov speling, liek 'difrənc' or 'difərənc', 'prefrənc' or 'prefərənc', 'shor' or 'shuer') Notes on theez toȯ chartz wil iméediətly foloe. **Lək up eny werd not fəly understəd** in a gəd dikshanəry, thə noetz əbúv, thə noetz foloeing, or in thə Glosəry az it bikúmz əváiləbəl. Thaer wil bee ə Soundzəbet in BI, foloed bẏ wun in AI. Arfter that, thaer wil bee ə rətúrn too Inglish (frunt paej) and IMS (bak).

Paej 2a (This paej is in Advárncd Inglish Maed Simpəl) (AI)

SOUNDZƏBET FOR BAESIK
INGLISH MAED SIMPƏL(BI)

(42 soundz/43 simbəlz)

sd	up/lo/alfəbet			sampəl Inglish werdz
01	Ə	ə	əh	bək, əlóu, serkəs, pət, atəm, kəd, ə, ənóid.
02	A	a	ak	hat, ant, malis, gras, at, hapy, an, plan.
03		ae	ae	haet, laezy, fael, aet, sae, pael, ae, maet.
04		air	air	air, fair, fairy, airəplaen, thair, tairing.
05		ar	ar	art, hart, grars, kar, char, marvələs, arm.
06	B	b	bee	bee, bed, baeby, bib, aebəl, skrub, tab.
07	Ch	ch	chae	cheez, church, mach, ich, chois, hachit.
08	D	d	dee	dot, didúkshən, did, ad, ded, padəl, deer.
09	E	e	ek	net, les, entry, pek, egz, leter, əléktrik.
10		ee	ee	leed, heed, eevən, heer, peek, tee, eegəl.
11		er	er	herd, fern, merder, bern, per, vers, erl.
12	F	f	ef	fat, difphong, frendly, infloe, Frans, of.
13	G	g	gae	drag, goetz, gigəbiet, bag, gum, rug, grin.
14	H	h	hae	him, bihíend, hert, home, əhéd, hel, harm.
15	I	i	ik	pil, ink, phink, ridəld, it, kwit, Itəly, litəl.
16		ie	ie	pie, fiel, dəzíer, ietəm, admíer, Ie, ielənd.
17	J	j	jae	juj, baj, əjúst, Joon, majik, injúst, aej.
18	K	k	kae	kat, karmə, akshən, krisp, aeking, karn't.
19	L	l	el	əlíev, loly, oeld, help, livid, orl, pael, bely.
20	M	m	em	am, mirer, mom, mum, amp, ambəl, tiem.
21	N	n	en	never, run, nunery, arnt, kan, noe, spin.
22		ng/ŋ	ing	Inglənd, soŋ, fling, aŋker, bang, rung, aŋəl.

(sd = sound number; up = uper kaes; lo = lower kaes)

Baesik IMS Soundzəbet kəntínued

sd	up/lo/alfəbet			sampəl Inglish werdz
23	O	o	ok	on, oliv, troly, oner, hot, chop, holy, song.
24		oe	oe	loen, oenly, noet, toest, roed, koech, soel.
25		oi	oi	oil, boiz, oister, koin, perlóin, foist, soil.
26		oo	oo	soon, food, Joolíe, troo, booz, oost, fool.
27		or	or	or, tort, orə, fəlórn, dorn, morning, krorl.
28		ou	ou	out, outbound, kou, oul, nou, pout, shouerz.
29	P	p	pee	pet, paeper, apt, grapəl, plee, apəl, prəpáir.
30		ph	phee	phree, maphz, erph, phe'rapy, pheesis.
31	R	r	rae	ma'ry, prie, ratz, be'ry, rae, broun, kreed.
32	S	s	es	sit, skul, mas, səsínkt, soe, as, fars, mies.
33		sh	shae	mash, sheeld, shiver, ash, oeshən, shəd, shee.
34	T	t	tee	trie, atik, terky, triet, bent, at, tart, tȯo, akt.
35		th	thə	thə, then, rarther, thair, bother, thoe, uther.
36	U	u	uk	luky, unkəl, rut, must, uniən, untie, blunt.
37		ue	ue	uezd, ues, ueniən, Tuezdae, skue, uenikorn.
38	V	v	vee	vou, waev, vəríeəty, vivid, ov, uvən, əlíev.
39	W	w	wae	wet, worter, əwáe, wen, hwen, wee, unwéd.
40/40	Ɏ	ɏ	ɏae	ɏeloe, ɏooph, biɏónd, ɏet, Tangənɏéekə.
10/41	Y	y	ɏy*	jely, narsty, nasty, hu'ry, so'ry, sily, taly.
41/42	Z	z	zed	zeebrə, maez, chikənz, zoo, az, pleez, antz.
42/43		zj	zjə	trezjer, mezjer, Aezjə, plezjer, dae zjə vóo.
(spaeser) '				lo'ry, port'hoel, ka'ry, po'rij, up'hoeld
ȧ ė ȯ u̇ (dot)				too, tȯo, toȯ (to, too, two)

(10/41 = sound/simbəl numberz) (*'yee')

SOUNDZƏBET FOR ADVANCD
INGLISH MAED SIMPƏL (AI)

(44 soundz/58 simbəlz)

sd/sm	up/lo/alfəbet			sampəl Inglish werdz
01/01	Ə	ə	əh	bək, əlów, cirkəs, pət, atəm, wəd, əták.
02/02	A	a	ak	at, gras, hapən, malic, ankəl, az, əbásh.
03/03		ae	ae	laet, haesty, graet, kaen, aep, raediənt.
04/04		aer	aer	faer, staer, Maery, kaer, dikláer, paer.
03/05		ai	ai	bait, strain, fail, rainz, plait, aim, strait.
04/06		air	air	air, dairy, airy, stair, fairly, airəplaen.
05/07		ar	ar	art, hart, grars, kar, army, ar, barterd.
06/08		au	au	taut, aurə, dauter, aul, aut, sauc, fraut.
06/09		aw	aw	awsəm, dawn, awning, saw, maw, klaw.
03/10		ay	ay	bay, paying, gray, slay, day, May, prayd.
07/11	B	b	bee	bed, krab, beating, aebəl, bib, babəl, tab.
08/12	C	c	cee	iec, cel, traec, niec, neec, cirkəs, iecikəl.
09/13		ch	chae	church, kach, choic, əchéev, chievz, lach.
10/14	D	d	dee	deed, tried, dieət, didúkshən, laid, ded.
11/15	E	e	ek	eg, tel, peny, entry, set, exit, eléktrik, elk.
12/16		ea	ea	eagəl, feast, eat, hear, cheat, pea, seat.
12/17		ee	ee	feet, beef, seen, beer, eery, heer, seemd.
13/18		er	er	ern, erly, murder, insért, flower, əmérj.
14/19	F	f	ef	fat, flý, frend, raft, rarft, of, əfar, fluf, if.
15/20	G	g	gae	green, hagəl, drag, gogəlz, goeing, gaej.
16/21	H	h	hae	hevən, bihíend, help, əhéd, port'hoel.
17/22	I	i	ik	ink, prity, milk, phin, qit, igloo, iritəbəl.
18/23		ie	ie	fiel, dəzíer, glieder, ielənd, iedəl, fienanc.
13/24		ir	ir	stir, fir, cirkəs, sir, wirl, shirk, flirt, irkd.
19/25	J	j	jae	juj, əjóin, baj, joodoe, majik, majəsty.
20/26	K	k	kae	kat, baekən, kiet, kichən, krischən, bak.
21/27	L	l	el	lik, haul, bawl, lemən, aul, lily, silikən.
22/28	M	m	em	am, mi'rer, mum, mom, saem, mimik.
23/29	N	n	en	never, runing, nany, nienty, antz, nun.

ȧ ė ȯ u̇ ẏ (dot) too/tȯo/toȯ (to/too/two). mẏ (my).

Advánccd IMS Soundzəbet kəntínued

sd/sm	up/lo/alfəbet			sampəl Inglish werdz
24/30		ng/ŋ	ing	**Iŋlish, song, piŋ, angəl, baŋ, angry, huŋ.**
25/31	O	o	ok	**hot, oter, onist, prod, foder, oliv, poty.**
26/32		oa	oa	**oak, boating, goal, loadəd, moan, toast.**
26/33		oe	oe	**oeld, toe, oeshən, voeter, boen, roezəry.**
27/34		oi	oi	**toil, koin, oil, void, soild, loiter, point.**
28/35		oo	oo	**mood, roost, soo, lood, boor, roof, roorəl.**
06/36		or	or	**fort, mor, porly, shor, or, fəlórn, tort.**
29/37		ou	ou	**foul, cloud, əlóud, out, flour, our, sound.**
29/38		ow	ow	**owl, klown, how, now, kow, powow, ow.**
27/39		oy	oy	**boy, joy, oyster, toy, employd, Roy.**
30/40	P	p	pee	**aep, pieper, apt, pop, əplíed, prəpáer.**
31/41		ph	phee	**breph, phree, maphz, parph, phink.**
32/42	Q	q	qae	**qiz, inqier, qosh, qeery, əqáint, qieət.**
33/43	R	r	rae	**run, roorəl, ror, raw, strip, krop, raer.**
08/44	S	s	es	**sitz, mos, moest, splay, sens, soe, baesəz.**
34/45		sh	shae	**shaev, trash, shee, ash, shəsh, smashing.**
35/46	T	t	tee	**teal, mat, tent, tried, metəl, tueter, satin.**
36/47		th	thə	**thə, then, thaer, thair, rarther, further.**
37/48	U	u	uk	**unkəl, tumbəl, rug, under, us, jut, hu'ry.**
38/49		ue	ue	**uez, ues, buety, Tuezday, nuez, uenifẏ.**
13/50		ur	ur	**urj, fur, urbən, murder, kurdəl, burnd.**
39/51	V	v	vee	**vien, viváeshəs, əlíev, hav, paevd, void.**
40/52	W	w	wae	**wax, əway, wen, əwáekən, wieder, wee.**
41/53	X	x	ex	**exit, fox, ax, oxen, maximəm, exəciez.**
42/54	Y̶	y̶	y̶ae	**y̶ot, biy̶ónd, y̶el, y̶earz, y̶eloe, y̶ak, y̶ard.**
12/55	Y	y	y̶y (yee)	**jely, nasty, hu'ry, so'ry, sily, jentry, aly.**
18/56	Ẏ	ẏ	y̶ẏ (yie)	**mẏ, pẏthon, flẏ, Ẏvən, tẏr, jẏrəskoep.**
43/57	Z	z	zed	**zeebrə, dayz, zoo, az, pleaz, eazy, hoez.**
44/58		zj	zjə	**trezjur, vizjən, Aezjə, dicízjən, seezjur.**

gráedəd, əlármd, inkrédibəl, wú'ry, əmérjəncy (main stres)

IMS is written as it sounds and spoken as it is written. Put another way, **both Basic IMS (BI) and Advancd IMS (AI) are written phonetically.** BI is simpler, in that it has practically no options to chose from: only one way to write the 'er' sound for example. However, the #10 'ee' has two options: **ee** or **y.** One keeps any choices close to the traditional English **(trad Eng)** spelling where practical. In this case, the trad Eng custom of using **y** for an **ee** sound at the end of a word like **jelly, dolly, ferry, dairy, photography,** is retained in both BI and AI, and can be used for the plural too, adding **'z'** to the **'y'.** When the **ee** sound is at the beginning or the middle of the word, it is more likely to be written **ee** in BI, or a choice of **ee/ea** in AI, depending on which letters were used in trad Eng. (Say this as it looks: **'trad eng'**)

Now AI **does** have choices for many vowel sounds, and also for the 's' sound, with a second choice of 'c'. Pick the nearest AI spelling to traditional English, such as **aec** for 'ace', or **sel** for 'sell'. (In BI the word is **aes**) In both BI and AI, the 'k' sound is only **'k'** **(kae)**, and not **'c' (cee)**, because the 'c' is designated as having an 'es' sound in AI.

BI has no c, q, or x, because you can make those sounds with **s, k, kw, ks, gz,** etc. However, **BI** does have **Ch, ch. Even though you may only use one form of IMS, such as AI, you should still review and understand the other form as well.** The world could pick one and discard the other, or two countries could make two different choices. Basic IMS is the simplest version, but this means that quite a few words sounding the same, would also be written the same way, except for adding an accent mark, like an extra dot on the vowel. AI avoids this, at a price: One needs to choose which version to write for that vowel sound, such as **ae, ai, ay.** Before IMS, simple dialects like pidgin English have already been favoured in more than a couple of countries. **Wikepedia shows about 30 pidgin English dialects around the world (2020). It is this author's opinion that BI is much more precise and universal than any existing version of pidgin English.**

Basic IMS has **42 sounds** and **43 symbols.** The only choice is discussed above. The numbers on the left refer to the sound and symbol, until we reach #40. Then the **41st** symbol **(y)** has the same sound as **#10 (ee).**

Advanced IMS has **44 sounds** and **58 symbols.** The two extra sounds are **q** and **x.** Several vowel sounds have two or three choices in AI like **ae/ai/ay, aer/air, au/aw/or, ea/ee/y, er/ir/ur, ie/ẏ, oa/oe, oi/oy, ou/ow.** One picks the nearest AI sounds and symbols to the trad Eng spelling. In this way, Advanced Inglish Maed Simpəl looks more familiar to traditional English users, but still writes and reads phonetically. (y̧ is strictly a consonant, **y** is strictly a vowel; use **y** for **ay/oy**)

IMS <u>iz</u> ritən az it soundz and spoekən az it iz ritən. Pət ənuther waɣ, **boeph Baesik IMS (BI) and Adváncd/Advárncd IMS (AI) ar ritən fənétikəly.** BI iz simpler, in that it haz praktikəly noe opshənz too chooz from: oenly wun waɣ too riet thee **'er'** sound for igzármpəl. Houévér, thə **# 10 'ee'** haz toò opshənz: **ee** or **y.** Wun keepz eny choisəz kloes too thə tradíshənəl Inglish **(trad Eng)** speling wair praktikəl. In this kaes, thə trad Eng custəm ov uezing **y** for an **ee** sound at thee end ov ə werd like **jely, doly, fery, dairy, fətógrəfy,** iz ritáend in boeph BI and AI, and kan bee uezd for thə ploorəl tòo, ading 'z' too the 'y'. Wen thee **ee** sound iz at thə bəgíning or thə midəl ov thə werd, it iz more liekly too bee ritən **ee** in BI, or ə chois ov **ee/ae** in AI, dipénding on wich leterz ar uezd in trad Eng. (Sae this az it ləks: **'trad eng'**)

Nou AI <u>duz</u> hav choisəz for meny vowəl soundz, and orlsoe for thee **'s'** sound, with ə sekənd choic ov **'c'.** Pick thə neerest AI speling too trad Eng, such az **aec** for 'ace' or **sel** for 'sell'. (In BI thə werd iz **aes**) In both BI and AI, thə **'k'** sound iz oenly **'k' (kae),** and not **'c' (cee),** bikóz thə **'c'** iz dezignaetəd az having an **'es'** sound in AI.

BI haz <u>no</u> c, q, or x, bikóz yoo kan maek thoez soundz with **s, k, kw, ks, gz,** etsetərə (ets.). Houévér, **BI** duz hav **Ch, ch. Even thoe yoo mae oenly uez wun form ov IMS, such az AI, yoo shəd stil rivúe and understánd thee uther form az wel.** Thə werld kəd pik wun and diskárd thee uther, or toò kunchryz kəd maek toò diferənt choisəz. Baesik IMS is thə simplist vershən, but this meenz that qiet ə fue werdz sounding thə saem wəd orlsoe bee ritən thə saem wae, eksépt for ading an aksənt mark, like an ekstrə dot on thə vouəl. AI avoidz this at a pries: wun needz too chooz wich vershən too riet for that vouəl sound, such az: **ae, ai, ay.** Bifór IMS, simpəl dieəlektz like pijin Inglish hav orlrédy been faeverd in mor than ə kupəl ov kunchryz. **Wikəpéediə shoez əbout 30 pijin Inglish dieəlektz əround thə werld (2020). It iz this orther'z əpíniən that BI iz much mor prəsíes and uenivérsəl** than eny igzísting vershən ov pijin Inglish.

Baesik IMS haz 42 soundz and 43 simbəlz. Thee oenly chois iz diskúsd əbúv. Thə numberz on thə left rəfér too thə sound and simbəl, until we reach #40. Then thə **41**st simbəl **(y)** haz thə saem sound az **#10 (ee).**

Advárnsd IMS haz 44 soundz and 58 simbəlz. Thə toò ekstrə soundz ar **q** and **x.** Severəl vouəl soundz hav toò or phree choisəz in AI, like **ae/ai/ay, aer/air, au/aw/or, ea/ee/y, er/ir/ur, ie/ẏ, oa/oe, oi/oy, ou/ow.** Wun piks thə neerest AI soundz and simbəlz too thə trad Eng speling. In this wae, Advárnsd Inglish Maed Simpəl lookz mor fəmíliər too trədíshənəl Inglish uezerz, but stil rietz and reedz fənétikəly. (ɣ is striktly ə konsənənt; **y** iz striktly ə vouəl; uez **y** for **ay/oy**)

The 'soft' or 'short' form of vowels **a, e, i, o, u** are hard to say on their own with any precision and need to be differentiated from their 'hard' or 'long' form: **ae, ee, ie, oe, ue.** So we add an easily pronounced letter **k** to the soft vowels, to put them in ABC mode as follows: **ak, ek, ik, ok, uk.** If you use 'okay', use it this way with four letters, or 'OK' in capitals, and bear in mind that **ok** is also the number 40 in Numberz Simplified, covered later.

The only vowel sounds with more than two letters are **aer/air**. Shortening to 'ai' or 'aa' was tried, but did not work well. Even with the shorter vowel, the 'r' was still needed on many words, such as 'dairy' or 'staering'. Dropping the 'r' also cut down on AI options for the 'ae' sound, and 'aa' is convenient but too foreign for English or IMS. All in all, **'air'** works well for BI, and **aer/air** for AI. While a few accents might sound the **'r'** of **aer/air**, most will only sound it as follows: **fairy/waery**, but not **fairly/baerly**. So **ae/ai** are the **'ae' sound (03)**, but **aer/air** are the **'air' sound (04)**. (air/aer take preference over ai/ae)

At the bottom of the soundsabet charts, **dots on top of vowels** are shown, excluding the normally dotted 'i'. This is a simple way to distinguish identically written words of different meanings for both BI and AI, by always dotting one particular vowel, as shown in the **'too/tȯo/toȯ'** example. Also seen here: a dot on top of a **'y'** changes the sound to **'ie'** in AI, which is sound/symbol 18/56 (ẏ). The **acute accent marks on vowels (á, é, í, ó, ú, ý)** are used on the **most stressed syllable of a word**, shown at the end of the AI soundsabet. **As English words are <u>usually</u> stressed on the first syllable, it was decided to apply the acute accent in all <u>other</u> cases, going back to the first page in IMS.** A forthcoming publication of a **word list or dictionary for IMS** will incorporate the use of these **dots**, along with **spelling** and the **primary word stress**, for **BI and AI**.

Note the changes from the trad Eng alphabet to the soundsabet alphabet (əh to **zjə)**, such as **gae, hae, rae, wae,** for more accuracy and better differentiation of the exact sound. Note, too, several newcomers like **əh, chae, ing, phee, shae, thə, ɣae, ɣee,** in both BI and AI, plus **ɣie** in AI only. Read **ɣae, ɣee, ɣie** as **yae, yee, yie,** using the trad Eng **'y'**, used here to show pronunciation only. In IMS we use the **'ɣ' (ɣae)** to get the consonant **'y'** sound; a **'y' (ɣy)** in IMS is a vowel sounded **'ee'**. The **ɣ (ɣae)** comes just before the **'y' (ɣy)** on the soundsabet. In development, this symbol has sometimes been closer to a modified **'j'** without the dot; either way, it ends up with the sound of a **consonant 'y' (ɣae** in IMS, **wye** in trad Eng). The UK **'zed'** was adopted over the US **'zee'**, purely because the latter is more easily confused with **cee, dee,** etc. when spoken.

Thə 'soft' or 'short' form ov vowəlz **a, e, i, o, u** ar hard too say on thair oen with eny prəcízjən and need too bee diferénshiaetəd from thair 'hard' or 'long' form: **ae, ee, ie, oe, ue.** So wee ad an easəly prənóuncd leter **k** too thə soft vowəlz, too pət them in ABC mode az foloez: **ak, ek, ik, ok, uk.** Shortən 'oekae/oekay' (BI/AI) too 'OK' in kapitəlz, and baer in miend that 'ok' iz aulsoe 40 in Numberz Simplified, kuverd laeter.

Thee oenly vowəl soundz with mor than toȯ leterz ar **aer/air.** Shortəning too 'ai' or 'aa' woz tried, but did not werk wel. Eevən with thə shorter vowəl, thə 'r' woz stil needəd on meny werdz, such az 'dairy' or 'staering'. Droping thee 'r' aulsoe kut down on AI opshənz for thee 'ae' sound, and 'aa' iz kənvéeniənt but too fo'rin for trad Eng or IMS. Aul in aul, **'air'** werkz wel for BI, and **'aer/air'** for AI. Wiel ə fue akcəntz miet sound thə **'r'** ov **aer/air**, moest wil oenly sound it az foloez: **fairy/waery**, but not **fairly/baerly.** Soe **ae/ai** ar thee **'ae' sound (03)**, but **aer/air** ar thee **'air' sound (04).** (air/aer taek prefrənc oever ai/ae)

At thə botəm ov thə soundzəbet chartz, **dotz on top ov vowəlz** ar shoen, exklóoding thə norməly dotəd 'i'. This iz ə simpəl waɣ too distíngwish iedéntikəly ritən werdz ov diferənt meaningz for boeph BI and AI, bý aulwaɣz doting wun pətíkueler vowəl, az shown in thə **too/tȯo/toȯ** exármpəl. Aulsoe seen heer: ə dot on top ov ə **'y'** chaenjəz thə sound too **'ie'** in AI, wich iz sound/simbəl 18/56 **(ẏ).** Thee əkúet aksənt markz on vowəlz **(á, é, í, ó, ú, ý)** ar uezd on thə **moest strest siləbəl ov ə werd**, shoen at thee end ov thee AI soundzəbet. **Az Inglish werdz ar** <u>uezuəly</u> **stresd on thə first siləbəl, it woz dicíedəd too əplý thee əkúet akcənt in aul** <u>uther</u> **kaesəz, goeiŋ bak too thə first paej ov IMS.** A forphkuming publikáeshən ov ə **werd list or dikshənəry for IMS** wil inkórpəraet thə ues ov theez **dotz**, əlong with **speling** and thə **priem>ry werd stres** for **BI and AI.**

Noet thə chaenjəz from thə trad Eng alfəbet too thə soundzəbet alfəbet (əh too **zjə)**, such az **gae, hae, rae, wae,** for mor akuerəcy and beter diferenshiáeshən ov thee exakt sound. Noet, too, severəl nuekumerz like **əh, chae, ing, phee, shae, thə, ɣae, ɣee,** in boeph BI and AI, plus **ɣie** in AI oenly. Read **ɣae, ɣee, ɣie** az **yae, yee, yie**, uezing thə trad Eng **'y'**, uezd heer too shoe prənunciáeshən oenly. In IMS wee uez thə **'ɣ' (ɣae)** too get thə konsənənt **'y'** sound; a **'y' (ɣy)** in IMS iz ə vowəl soundəd **'ee'.** Thə **'ɣ' (ɣae)** kumz just bəfor thə **'y' (yee)** on thə soundzəbet. In divéləpmənt, this simbəl haz sumtiemz been kloeser too ə modified **'j'** without thə dot; iether way, it endz up with thə sound ov ə **konsənənt 'y'** (yae in IMS, **wye** in trad Eng). Thə UK **'zed'** woz ədóptəd oever thə US **'zee'**, puerly bikóz thə later iz mor eazəly konfuezd with **cee, dee,** etc. wen spoekən.

To enable a smoother transition from trad Eng to IMS, **the ABC format has been retained, inserting new sounds or symbols in alphabetical order.** So **'ə' (əh)** starts off the soundsabet; it is, after all, the commonest 'a' sound and takes its place just ahead of **'a' (ak).** The **'zj' (zjə)** sound is not widely used in English/Inglish (trezjer/trezjur BI/AI) but it is a smaller part of the widely used **'j' (jae)** sound. While it does have a separate symbol for the 'zj', **the International Phonetic Alphabet (IPA) does not parallel IMS or have the look and feel of the English language for the most part.** The schwa **'ə' (əh)** is an obvious exception.

Occasionally there are regional accent/dialect choices, but, most of the time one regional accent will be written exactly as another. Of note is the **alternate spelling for 'grass' as 'grars' or 'gras',** with the **'r' sound** being prevalent in **southern England** and parts of northeastern North America, while the **'a' sound** is standard in **northern England** and other parts of the UK, Ireland, USA and Canada. These two dialects can be designated as ***S** (grars) and ***N** (gras). You will see IMS written in this manual with both dialects, including 'Adváncd/Advárncd' and 'Advâncd' (explained two paragraphs ahead). The basic or default pronunciation for IMS is primarily that used in southern England, like most Oxford English dictionaries found on both sides of the Atlantic. However, read again the first sentence of this paragraph: **IMS wants you to keep your accent!**

Another regional difference is with 'ue' ('yoo' in trad Eng). Some accents, including much of the USA, lose the **y/ɣ** (trad Eng/IMS) on certain words, replacing the vowel sound with a simple **'oo'.** Examples are: **duety/dooty, aptitued/aptitood, astuet/astoot.** But **buety, muet, huemid, and many others,** are standard on both sides of the Atlantic. Other regions like Cockney/East End (of London, UK) also drop the **y/ɣ,** but more indiscriminately.

If you are well schooled in your regional accent, feel free to write it as you say it, using the soundsabets as your guide/template. That said, an alternate handling for the ***S/*N dialects** and the **USA 'ue/oo' situation** is being introduced in time for the 2020 first edition printing. **A circumflex/caret (^) on the vowel indicates alternate sounds according to one's dialect.** Thus, **'Advâncd'** is pronounced with **'ar' or 'a'** for the second 'a' **(â).** **'Dûety'** would be **'duety' or 'dooty'** according to your accent/location. Obviously one must prioritize whether one adds a **dot,** a **caret,** or an **acute accent;** in AI the dot on the 'y' **(ẏ)** is a clear soundsabet priority (as in **aplẏ);** in most cases the caret would trump the acute accent (as in **advâncd),** unless taking an alternative (**advárncd, advárncd**). Either way, be consistant for the whole text, except when learning.

Note that 'iə' is a short cut for 'eeə', provided the 'ee' sound is kept relatively short. This parallels common English useage. **On its own, the 'i' is soft, as in 'hit', but combined with 'ə' and other vowels, it retains a short 'ee' sound.**

Too enáebəl ə smoother tranzíshən from trad Eng too IMS, **thee ABC format haz been rətáend, insérting new soundz or simbəlz in alfəbétikəl order.** Soe '**ə**' (**əh**) startz of thə soundzəbet; it iz, âfter aul, thə komənist 'a' sound and taekz its plaec just əhed ov '**a**' (**ak**). The '**zj**' (**zjə**) sound iz not wiedly uezd in trad Eng/Inglish (trezjer/trezjur BI/AI), but iz ə smauler part ov thə wiedly uezd '**j**' (**jae**) sound. Wiel it duz hav ə sepərət simbəl for thə 'zj', **thə Internáshənəl Fənétik Alfəbet (IPA/IFA) duz not pa'rəlel IMS or hav thə lək and feel ov thee Inglish langwij** for thə moest part. Thə shwar '**ə**' (**əh**) iz an obviəs excépshən.

Əkáezjənəly thaer ar reejənəl akcənt/dieəlekt choicəz, but, moest ov thə tiem wun reejənəl akcənt wil bee ritən exáktly az ənúther. Ov noet iz thee **aultérnətiv speling for 'grass' az 'grars' or 'gras',** with thə '**r**' **sound** beeing prevələnt in **suthən Ingländ** and partz ov norphéastən Norph Əmé'rikə, wiel thee '**a**' **sound** iz standerd in **northən Ingländ** and uther partz ov thə UK, Ierlənd, USƏ and Canədə. Theez toò dieəlektz kan bee dezignaetəd az ***S** (grars) and ***N** (gras). Yoo wil see IMS ritən in this manueəl with boeph dieəlektz, inklóoding Adváncd, Advárncd and Advâncd (expláind toò pa'rəgrâfz əhed). Thə baesik or difáult prənunciáeshən ov IMS iz priemé'rily that uezd in suthən Ingländ, liek moest Oxfəd dikshənəryz found on boeph siedz ov thee Atlántik. Howéver, read əgain thə first sentənc ov this pa'rəgrâf: **IMS wontz yoo too keep yor aksənt!**

Ənúther reejənəl difrənc iz with 'ue' (yoo in trad Eng). Sum akcəntz, inklóoding moest ov thee USƏ, looz thə y/ɣ (trad Eng/IMS), rəpláecing thə vowəl sound with ə simpəl '**oo**'. Exâmpəlz ar: **duety/dooty, aptitued/aptitood, astuet/astoot.** But **buety, muet, huemid, and meny utherz,** ar standerd on boeph siedz ov thee Atlántik. Uther reejənz like Kokny/East End (ov Lundən, UK) aulsoe drop thə y/ɣ, but mor indiskríminətly.

If yoo ar wel skoold in yor reejənəl aksənt, feel free too riet it az yoo say it, uezing thə soundzəbetz az yor gied/templaet. That sed, an aultérnətiv handling for thə *S/*N **dialekts** and thə **USƏ 'ue/oo' situeáeshən** iz beeing intrədúecd in tiem for thə 2020 first idíshən printing. **A cirkəmflex/ka'rət (^) on thə vowəl indikaetz aultérnətiv soundz, akórding to wun'z dieəlekt.** Thus, '**Advâncd**' iz prənóuncd with '**ar**' or '**a**' for thə sekənd 'a' (**â**). '**Dûety**' wəd bee '**duety**' or '**dooty**' əkórding too yor aksənt/loekáeshən. Obviəsly wun must prieó'rityz wether wun adz ə **dot**, ə **ka'rət**, or an **əkúet aksənt**; in AI thə dot on thə 'y' (**ẏ**) iz ə klear soundzəbet prieó'rity (az in **aplẏ**); in moest kaesəz thə ka'rət wəd trump thee əkúet akcənt (az in **advâncd**), unles taeking an aultérnətiv (**adváncd, advárncd**). Iether way, bee konsístənt for thə hoel text, ixcépt wen lerning.

Noet that 'iə' iz ə short kut for 'eeə', prəvíedəd thee 'ee' iz kept relətivly short. This pa'rəlelz komən trad Eng uesij. **On itz oen, thee 'i' iz soft az in 'hit', but kombíend with 'ə' and uther vowəlz, it ritáinz ə short 'ee' sound.**

Paej 7a (This paej iz in Advâncd Inglish Maed Simpəl) (AI)

Most of the time you will write the same way, with even widely different accents, because the same soundsabet letters will have a different sound to you. Writers with accents closer to what most national or international broadcasting stations are using, will be able to express the exact sound of a regional accent by using IMS phonetically. Yes, it is already phonetic, but think of today or before IMS, how a writer would try to approximate an accent: often it falls flat because **the 'a' is 'ar' to the Londoner, 'air' to the Angelino (LA), 'a' to the Liverpudlian (think Beatles), 'arr' to the Bostonian, 'ə' to the UK Midlands, and so forth,** not forgetting that many African countries use English in an official capacity with their own accents. **IMS gives the writer more control over what the reader reads and how it sounds.**

So what about letter combinations like **gl, kt, mp, nd, iə, sp, mb, nt, bl, lb, sm, pl, lp, ft, lk, st, ld, zd, sl, kw, ks, tz and others?** Should they have their own place in the soundsabets? No, this is not necessary, since they work as they are, two letters spoken next to each other and already in the soundsabets as their separate selves. **The diphthongs included in the soundsabets like ch, ng, ph, sh, th, zj, and many vowel sounds other than a, e, i, o, u, are not obvious, like the combinations above.** Making a list of all two-letter sound combinations in Inglish could be a fruitful learning exercise, but we will keep the soundsabets at their current simpler length of 43/58 symbols for BI/AI.

It is tempting to add **'ear/eer' and 'ier'** to the **vowel sounds,** but they are obvious enough to leave out of the soundsabets, once you apply the **rule that a soundsabet takes preference over other letters, unless broken up by a spacer.** Before printing the 2020 first edition, the author has been using single quotation marks for spacers. However, while quotation marks will work for now, using proportional fonts,* **the marks for a spacer should take up no more than half the space of an average vowel. It should be either a straight vertical line or a straight inverted teardrop**, at the same location as the single quotation mark. Prior to publishing, a point-down pip from Word © (') is doing a better job, but getting these symbols on one's keyboard is an early goal. (*each character occupies only as much width as it needs)

The 'th' as in 'thə' ('the' in trad Eng) **stays the same; 'th' as in 'three' is a slightly different sound and takes 'ph' or 'phee'.** Remember it with **phree/three** in IMS/trad Eng. The **'ph'** has been a diphthong for the 'f' (ef) sound in trad Eng, but we have no need of a second 'f' (ef) in IMS, so **get used to using 'ph' for the voiced 'th' sound.** Once you get used to spelling **'difphong'** this way, you will never have trouble spelling that word again!

Moest ov thə tiem yoo wil riet thə saem wae, with eevən wiedly difrənt aksəntz, bikóz thə saem soundzəbet leterz wil hav ə difrənt sound too yoo. Rieterz with aksəntz kloeser too wot moest nashənəl or internáshənəl brordkâsting staeshənz ar uezing, wil bee aebəl too ikspres thee igzakt sound ov ə reejənəl aksənt bie uezing IMS fənétikəly. Yes, it iz orlrédy fənétik, but phink ov toodáe or bifór IMS, hou ə riter wəd trie too əpróksəmaet an aksənt: ofən it forlz flat bikóz **thee 'a' iz 'ar' too thə Lundəner, 'air' too thee Anjəléenoe (LA), 'a' too thə Liverpúdliən (phink Beetəlz), 'arr' too thə Bostóeniən, 'ə' too thə UK Midləndz, and soe forph,** not fəgéting that meny Afrikən kunchryz uez Inglish in an əfíshəl kəpásity with thair oun aksəntz. **IMS givz thə rieter mor kəntróel oever wot thə reeder reedz and hou it soundz.**

Soe wot əbout leter kombináeshənz like gl, kt, mp, nd, iə, sp, mb, nt, bl, lb, sm, pl, lp, ft, lk, st, ld, zd, sl, kw, ks, tz and utherz? Shəd thae hav thair oen plaes in thə soundəbetz? Noe, this iz not nesəsəry, sins thae werk az thae ar, toȯ leterz spoekən nekst too eech uther and orlrédy in thə soundzəbetz az thair sepərət selvz. **Thə difphongs inklóodəd in thə soundzəbetz like ch, ng, ph, sh, th, zj, and meny vouəl soundz uther than a, e, i, o, u, ar not obviəs, like thə kombináeshənz əbúv.** Maeking ə list ov orl toȯ-leter sound kombináeshənz in Inglish kəd bee ə frootfəl lerning eksəsiez, but wee wil keep thə soundzəbetz at thair kurənt simpler length ov 43/58 simbəlz for BI/AI.

It iz tempting too ad **'ear/eer' and 'ier'** too thə **vouəl soundz,** but thae ar obviəs inuf too leev out ov thə soundzəbetz, wuns yoo əplíe thə **rool that ə soundzəbet taekz preferəns oever uther leterz, unles broekən up bie ə spaeser.** Bifor printing thə 2020 ferst ədishən, thee orpher haz been uezing singəl kwoetáeshən marks for spaeserz. Houever,* wiel kwoetáeshən markz wil werk for nou, uezing prəpórshənəl fontz, **thə markz for ə spaeser shəd taek up noe mor than hâf thə spaes ov an avərij vouəl. It shəd bee iether ə straet vertikəl lien or ə straet invértəd teerdrop,** at thə saem loekáeshən az thə singəl kwoetáeshən mark. Prieər too publishing, ə point-doun pip from Werd © (') iz dooing ə beter job, but geting theez simbəlz on wun'z keebord iz an erly goel. (*reed az 'ou+e' bikóz 'ou' iz bifór 'ue')

Thə 'th' az in 'thə' ('the' in trad Eng) **staez thə saem; 'th', az in 'three', iz ə slietly difrənt sound and taekz 'ph' or 'phee'.** Rəmémber it with **phree/three** in IMS/trad Eng. Thə **'ph'** haz been ə difphong for thə 'f' (ef) sound in trad Eng, but wee hav noe need ov ə sekənd 'f' in IMS, soe **get uezd too uezing 'ph' for thə voisd 'th' sound.** Wuns yoo get uezd too spelling **'difphong'** this way, yoo wil never hav trubəl speling that werd əgén!

In Old English, around 900 AD, these two 'th' sounds correctly had different symbols: þ (alt+0254) as thorn ('phorn' in IMS/θ* in IPA) for three/phree, maths/maphz, or thing/phing; and ð (alt+0240) as edh or eth (ð in IPA). Thorn was written like a 'b' on top of a 'p'; we keep the 'p' and write it 'ph' (phee). Eth was a circle with a wind-blown cross on top, recently revived by the International Phonetic Alphabet; we will stay with the 'th' (thə) for rather/râther, other/uther or then. On saying 'thə' ('the' in trad Eng), notice how you seal your upper teeth with your tongue, then pull your tongue away. Now say 'phree' ('three' in trad Eng). While your tongue is close to your upper teeth, it pulls back and more air is pushed forwards. The difference is subtle but clear, like red wine and rosé. Also note that the phree phingy we just did using a phee, is considered 'voiced' as compared to our 'thə' which is not. (*alt+952)

While on the subject of 'the/thə', you must have noticed how often it changes to 'thee', either as emphasis or in front of a vowel. Most English speakers have followed this rule since early childhood, but it is hardly noticed when you write the same 'the' all the time. Note, too, that a word starting with 'ue' should be treated as if it were a consonant, owing to its begining with the 'ɣ' (ɣae) sound. What applies to 'thə/thee' also applies to ə/an (ə kar/an ox), with 'ae' for emphasis. As stated before, if you really know your dialect, and your rules are different, be my guest. We write what we say in Inglish Maed Simpəl!

If you pronounce the 'h' (hae) in 'what' as 'hwot', as some Americans do, then write it that way. Otherwise write it as 'wot'. The 'h' (hae) is not silent in IMS, unless in a foreign word with original spelling, or at the end of a word, like 'əh', the first sound of the soundsabet. Sometimes in trad Eng the 'h' can act as a silent partner to an exclamation: Ah! Bah! Ugh! Oh! In this silent partnership, the 'h' always comes at the end. In IMS you can do it that way too, but let's see an end to 'an history'.

By now some of you will have noticed the frequent use of the soundzabet sound 'er' (ir/ur) in IMS, and compared it with the International Phonetic Alphabet use of 'ə' and 'ər'. IMS is grateful for the shwa ('əh' in BI and AI), but also keeps the flavour of English, which includes a continued wide use of 'er' (ir/ur) and also 'ar' and 'or' (au/aw). Depending where it occurs, there is not a lot of difference between 'er', 'ər' and 'ə'. However, go by the soundsabets and their diphthongs; these can be broken up with a spacer; 'ər' is <u>not</u> an automatic diphthong like 'er', but can sometimes be used, such as 'lieər', instead of 'lie'er'. The IPA/IFA symbols have been added to the Soundsabet on pages 19-19a, to improve understanding, not to substitute for the BI or AI symbols; in some cases they are approximate matches only.

In Oeld Inglish, əróund 900 AD, theez toȯ 'th' soundz kəréktly had difərənt (difrənt*) simbəlz: þ (alt+0254) az thorn ('phorn' in IMS/θ in IFA) for three/phree, maths/maphz, or thing/phing; and ð (alt+0240) as edh or eth (ð in IFA). Thorn woz ritən liek ə 'b' on top ov ə 'p'; wee keep thə 'p' and riet it 'ph' (phee). Eth woz ə serkəl with ə wind-bloen kros on top, reesəntly rəvíevd bie thee Internáshənal Fənetik Alfəbet; wee wil stae with thə 'th' (thə) for rather/râther, other/uther or then. On saeing 'thə' ('the' in trad Eng), noetis hou yoo seel ɣor uper teeph with yor tung, then pəl yor tung əwáe. Nou sae 'phree' ('three' in trad Eng). Wiel yor tung iz kloes too yor uper teeph, it pəlz bak and mor air iz pəshd forwədz. Thə diferəns iz sutəl but kleer, like red wien and roezáe. Orlsoe noet that thə phree phingy wee just did uezing a phee, iz kənsíderd 'voisd' az kəmpáird too our 'thə' wich iz not. (*toȯ siləbəl opshən)

Wiel on thə subjekt ov 'the/thə', yoo must hav noetisd hou ofən it chaenjəs too 'thee', iether az emfəsis or in frunt ov ə vouəl. Moest Inglish speekerz hav foloed this rool sins erly chieldhəd, but it iz hardly noetisd wen yoo riet thə saem 'the' orl thə tiem. Noet too, that ə werd starting with 'ue' shəd bee treetəd az if it wer ə konsənənt, oeing too itz bəgining with thə 'ɣ' (ɣae) sound. Wot əpliez too 'thə/thee', orlsoe əpliez too 'ə/an' (ə kar/an oks), with 'ae' for emfəsis. Az staetəd bifór, if yoo reely noȯ yor dieəlekt, and yor roolz ar difərənt, bee mie gest. Wee riet wot wee sae in Inglish Maed Simpəl!

If yoo prənóuns thə 'h' (hae) in 'what', az 'hwot', az sum Əmé'rikənz doo, then riet it that wae. Utherwiez riet it az 'wot'. Thə 'h' iz not sielənt in IMS, unles in ə fo'rin werd with əríjinəl speling, or at thee end ov ə werd, like 'əh', thə ferst sound ov thə soundzəbet. Sumtiemz in trad Eng, thə 'h' kan akt az ə sielənt partner too an eksklamáeshən: Âh! Bâh! Ugh! Oh! In this sielənt partnership, thə 'h' orlwaez kumz at thee end. In IMS yoo kan doo it that wae tȯo, but letz see an end too 'an histery'.

Bie nou sum ov yoo wil hav noetisd thə freekwənt ues ov thə soundzəbet sound 'er' (ir/ ur) in IMS, and kəmpáird it with thə Internáshənəl Fənétik Alfəbet ues ov 'ə' and 'ər'. IMS is grateful for thə schwa (əh in BI and AI), but orlsoe keepz thə flaever ov Inglish, wich inklóodz ə kontínued wied ues ov 'er' (ir/ur) and orlsoe 'ar' and 'or' (au/ aw). Dəpending on wair it əkerz, thair iz not ə lot ov diferəns bətwéen 'er', 'ər' and 'ə'. Houever, goe bie thə soundzəbets and thàir difphongz; theez kan bee broekən up with ə spaeser; 'ər' iz not an ortəmatik difphong like 'er', but kan sumtiemz bee uezd, such az 'lieər', insted ov 'lie'er'. Thee IPA/IFA simbəlz hav been adəd too thə Soundzəbet on pages 19-19a, too impróov understánding, not too substituet for thə BI or AI simbəlz; in sum kaesəz thae ar əpróksəmət machəz oenly.

READING AND WRITING IN INGLISH MÆD SIMPƏL:

(trad Eng) After reading the soundsabet for Inglish Maed Simpəl, it is important to read a paragraph or three in IMS, to see exactly how it's done, and how the soundsabet letters are being used to get the correct spelling and pronunciation. Here are some paragraphs in English, Basic IMS and Advanced IMS. If the meaning or pronunciation is not obvious, look it up in the appropriate soundsabet.

(BI) Arfter reeding thə soundzəbet for Inglish Maed Simpəl, it iz importənt too reed ə pa'rəgrarf or phree in IMS, too see igzaktly hou it'z dun, and hou thə soundzəbet leterz ar beeing uezd too get thə kərekt speling and prənunsiaeshən. Heer ar sum pa'rəgrarfz in Inglish, Baesik IMS and Advarnsd IMS. If thə meening or prənunsiaeshən iz not obviəs, lək it up in thee əproepriət soundzəbet.

(AI) After reading thə soundzəbet for Inglish Maed Simpəl, it iz importənt too read ə pa'rəgraf or phree in IMS, too see ixaktly how it'z dun, and how thə soundzəbet leterz ar beeing uezd too get thə kərekt speling and prənunciaeshən. Heer ar sum pa'rəgrafz in Inglish, Baesik IMS and Advancd IMS. If thə meaning or prənunciaeshən iz not obviəs, lək it up in thee əproepriət soundzəbet.

Note that neither versions of IMS were longer than the traditional English. Some words are longer, but other words are shorter.

The **BI** version was written with **'ar' (*S dialect),** rather than **'a' (*N dialect)** in the **AI** version, for certain words like **after/advanced**. Which one is chosen is up to the writer, editor or publisher, and what the local dialect dictates. However, using a **caret (^)** on the **'a' (â),** as explained on page 7, will let the reader choose according to the dialect he uses, or is learning.

The **'ee' sound**, when short and mid-word, like **'prənunsiaeshən/obviəs'** above, can be reproduced in IMS with **'i'** (as in trad Eng). **The 'i' is shorter than 'ee' on the page and is so preferred.** Don't confuse this with the **'i' or 'ie'** in words like **did/flip or ried/iecikəl** (ride/icicle in trad Eng), which are sounded exactly per their soundsabet. Be aware of the **diphthong in the soundsabet, which takes preference, like 'ai/oi/th', unless divided by a spacer.**

(We will briefly pause on showing stressed syllables in IMS until page 13)

REEDING AND RIETING IN INGLISH MAED SIMPƏL:

Noet that niether vershənz ov IMS wer longer than trədishənəl Inglish. Sum werdz ar longer, but uther werdz ar shorter.

Thə **BI** vershən woz ritən with **'ar'** (***S dieəlekt**), rarther than **'a'** (***N dieəlekt**) in thee **AI** vershən for sertən werdz like **after/advanced**. Wich wun iz choezən iz up too thə rieter, editer or publisher, and wot thə loekəl dieəlekt diktaetz. Houever, uezing ə **ka'rət (^)** on thee **'a' (â)**, az eksplaend on paej 7, wil let thə reeder chooz, əkording too thə dieəlekt hee uezəz, or iz lerning.

Thee **'ee' sound**, wen short and mid-werd, like **'prənunsiaeshən/obviəs'** əbuv, kan bee reeprəduesd in IMS with **'i'** (as in trad Eng). **Thee 'i' (ik) iz shorter than 'ee' on thə paej and iz so prəferd.** Doen't konfuez this with thee **'i' (ik) or 'ie'** in werdz like **did/flip or ried/iesikl** (ride/icicle in trad Eng), wich ar soundəd igzaktly per thair soundzəbet. Bee əwair ov thə **difphong in thə soundzəbet, wich taekz preferəns, liek ae/oi/th, unles diviedəd bie ə spaeser.**

(Baesik IMS Abuv. <u>Advâncd IMS Bəloe.</u>)

READING AND RIETING IN INGLISH MAED SIMPƏL:

Noet that niether vershənz ov IMS wer longer than trədishənəl Inglish. Sum werdz ar longer, but uther werdz ar shorter.

Thə **BI** vershən woz ritən with **'ar'** (***S dieəlekt**), rarther than **'a'** (***N dieəlekt**) in thee **AI** vershən for certən werdz liek **after/advancd**. Wich wun iz choezən iz up too thə rieter, editer or publisher, and wot thə loekəl dieəlekt diktaetz. However, uezing ə **ka'ret (^)** on thee **'a' (â),** az explaind on paej 7, wil let thə reader chooz əkording too thə dieəlekt hee uezəs or iz lerning.

Thee **'ee' sound**, wen short and mid-werd, like **prənunciaeshən/obviəs** əbuv, kan bee reeprəduecd in IMS with **'i'** (as in trad Eng). **Thee 'i' (ik) iz shorter than 'ee' on thə paej and iz so prəferd.** Doen't konfuez this with **'i' (ik) or 'ie'** in werdz liek **did/flip or ried/iecikəl** (ride/icicle in trad Eng), wich ar soundəd ixaktly per thair soundzəbet. Bee əwaer ov thə **difphong in thə soundzəbet, wich taekz preferənc, liek ai/oi/th, unles diviedəd bẏ ə spaecer.**

(Wee wil breefly pauz on shoeing stresd siləbəlz in IMS until paej 13)

(BI) Janueəry 27, 1967

Jim Lovell (luvəl) woz having diner at thə Wiet Hous, wen hiz frend, Ed White (wiet) bernd too deph. Aktueəly, it wozn't reely diner Lovell woz having, just finger sandwichəz, o'rinj joos, and unmemərəbəl wien, laed out on linən-kuverd taebəlz in thə Green Room. Aktueəly tòo, Ed White didn't reely bern too deph. Thə fuemz klaemd him long bifor thə flaemz ever kəd hav.

(AI) Janueəry 27, 1967

Jim Lovell (luvəl) woz having diner at thə Wiet Hous, wen hiz frend, Ed White (wiet) burnd too deph. Aktueəly, it wozn't realy diner Lovell woz having, just finger sandwichəs, o'rinj jooc, and unmemərəbəl wien, laid out on linen-kuverd taebəlz in thə Green Room. Aktueəly too, Ed White didn't realy burn too deph. Thə fuemz klaimd him long bifor thə flaemz ever kəd hav.

Proper names like **Lovell** and **White** can be written in their original spelling, followed by the IMS spelling and pronunciation in parentheses, az **(luvəl)** and **(wiet)**; or write a place name similarly: **Vancouver (vankóover).** It is not compulsory, but **a good writer would do this the first time the proper name was used.** Future usage may adjust the spelling over to IMS, just as **Peking** became **'Beijing'** as a closer pronunciation for the western world. Of course, it is a cinch with IMS: no ambiguity with the soundsabets, as there is now, with the **'ei'** (**'ae'** perhaps, or **eether/iether**) and the **'j'** (**jae** or **zjə**) in **'Beijing'**.

Looking at **'sandwiches'**, we have three syllables: **'sand' 'wich' 'es'** becoming **'sand' 'wich' 'əz'** in IMS. Most of the time **we put a 'zed/zee' sound at the end of a word to make it plural,** and write it as an 's' (es). **Now we will write it the way it sounds, with a 'zed'.** And it is clearly **'əz'**, with a schwa, not 'ez' or 'es'. We do the same with the five syllables of **'unmemorable'** as **'un' 'mem' 'ə' 'rə' 'bəl'**. The ending **'le'** changes to **'əl'**, just like it sounds and becomes the fifth syllable. Note, however, the **'ed'** in **'burned, covered, claimed'**. These will **not get a vowel** because the **added consonant does not add a syllable.** So we keep **one** syllable for **bernd, burnd, klaemd** or **klaimd,** and **two** for **kuverd.**

Proper naemz liek **Lovell** and **White** kan bee ritən in thair ərijənəl speling, foloed bie thee IMS speling and prənunsiaeshən in pa'renphəseez, az: **(luvəl)** and: **(wiet)**; or riet ə plaes naem similəly: **Vancouver (vankóover).** It iz not kəmpulsəry, but **ə gəd rieter wəd doo this thə ferst tiem thə proper naem woz uezd.** Fuecher uesij mae əjust thə speling over to IMS, just az **Peking** bikaem **'Beijing'** az ə kloeser prənunsiaeshən for thə western world. Ov kors, it iz ə sinch with IMS: noe ambigueity with thə soundzəbets, az thair iz nou, with thə **'ei'** (**'ae'** perhaps, or **eether/iether**) and thə **'j'** (**jae** or **zjə**) in **'Beijing'**.

Ləking at **'sandwiches'**, wee hav phree siləbəlz: **'sand' 'wich' 'es'** bikuming **'sand' 'wich' 'əz'** in IMS. Moest ov thə tiem **wee pət ə zed/zee sound at thee end ov ə werd too maek it ploorəl,** and riet it az an 's' (es). Nou wee wil riet it thə wae it soundz, with ə 'zed'. And it iz kleerly **'əz',** with ə shwar, not 'ez' or 'es'. Wee doo thə saem with thə fiev siləbəlz ov **'unmemərəbəl'** az **'un' 'mem' 'ər' 'əb' 'əl'. Thee ending 'le' chaenjəz too 'əl', just like it soundz and inklooding thə fifph siləbəl.** Noet, houever, thee **'ed'** in **'burned, covered, claimed'. Theez wil not get a vouəl bikoz thee adəd konsənənt duz not ad ə siləbəl.** Soe wee keep wun siləbəl for **bernd/klaemd** and toȯ for **kuverd.**

(Baesik IMS Əbuv. Advâncd IMS Bəloe.)

Proper naemz like **Lovell** and **White** kan bee ritən in thair ərijinəl speling, foloed bẏ thee IMS speling and prənunciaeshən in pa'renphəseez, az **(luvəl)** and **(wiet)**; or riet ə plaec naem similəly: **Vancouver (vankoover).** It iz not kəmpulsəry, but **ə gəd rieter wəd doo this thə first tiem thə proper naem woz uezd.** Fuecher uesij may əjust thə speling over too IMS, just az **Peking bikaem 'Beijing' az ə kloeser prənunciaeshən for thə western world.** Of kors, it iz a cinch with IMS: noe ambigueity with thə soundzəbetz, az thaer iz now, with thə **'ei'** (**'ae'** perhaps, or **eether/iether**) and thə **'j'** (**jae** or **zjə**) in **'Beijing'**.

Ləking at **'sandwiches'**, wee hav 3 siləbəlz: **'sand' 'wich' 'es'** bikuming **'sand' 'wich' 'əz' in IMS.** Moest ov thə tiem **wee pət ə zed/zee sound at thəə end ov ə werd too maek it ploorəl,** and riet it az an 's' (es). **Now wee wil riet it thə way it soundz, with ə 'zed'.** And it iz klearly **'əz',** with ə shwar, not 'ez' or 'es'. Wee doo thə saem with thə fiev siləbəlz ov **'unmemərəbəl'** az **'un' 'mem' 'ə' 'rəb' 'əl'. Thee ending 'le'** chaenjəz too **'əl',** just like it soundz, and bikumz thə fifph siləbəl. Noet, however, thee **'ed'** in **'burned, covered, claimed'.** These wil **not get ə vowəl** bikoz thee **adəd konsənant duz not ad ə siləbəl.** Soe wee keep **wun** siləbəl for **bernd, burnd, klaemd** or **klaimd,** and **toȯ** for **kuverd.**

The next examples of BI and AI will show the **primary stressed vowel sounds** of each word that is two or more syllables long. **This will be shown by an acúte áccent on the first letter of the most stressed vowel sound in the word.** This section is included to further deliver on the promise of IMS being easier to pronounce over trad Eng. It will be included in any IMS Word Lists for Spelling, or Dictionaries.

(BI) Kórling Chuck (chuk) mae hav been mie intént, but lief intervéend. Mie wérking lief that iz. Ie'd been gon moest ov thee afternóon, but TenHuis (hies) Chocoláde (chokəláed) had been róking əlong. Bifór Ie korl énybody, Ie had too goe phroo ə piel ov mésijəz Ant Néttie (néty) had táekən hwiel I'd been gon. Moest ov them kəd waet, but Ie had too korl thə bank, then doo an ínvois for fiev poundz ov krem də monph bónbonz, that wəd ədórn thə píloez ov thə nue Grae Gáebəls Kónfərəns Sénter. Ant Néttie had orlrédy boksd them up. Ie'd dəlíver them on mie wae hoem.

(AI) Káuling Chuck (chuk) may hav been mẏ intént, but lief intervéend. Mẏ wérking lief that iz. I'd been gon moest ov thee arfternóon, but TenHuis (hies) Chocoláde (chokəláed) had been róking əlóng. Bifór I kaul énybody, I had too goe phroo ə piel ov mésijəz Arnt Néttie (néty) had táekən wiel I'd been gon. Moest ov them kəd wait, but I had too korl thə bank, then doo an ínvoic for fiev poundz ov krem də monph bónbonz, that wəd ədórn thə píloez ov thə nue Gray Gáebəlz Kónfərənc Cénter. Artnt Néttie had aulrédy boxd them up. I'd dəlíver them on mẏ way hoem.

This section through page 13 shows the stressed vowels for words of more than one syllable. You will see that **most words are stressed on the first syllable**, meaning that once we learn that lesson, we can skip this unnecessary step, and **simply accent syllables of primary stress that come second, third, or beyond.** A student or writer need not be obligated to always make these notations, but it will be encouraged in published works and re-publishing in IMS, particularly for new readers or ESL (English as a Second Language).

In trad Eng, the personal pronoun for oneself is 'I' (capital 'ie'). **In BI, we keep it phonetic with 'Ie'** (capital 'ie' + 'e'). **In AI, we use the 'I'** (capital 'ie') **and pronounce it 'ie',** a rare exception to the spell/prono rule.

This time we started with the ***N option for Ant Nettie in BI**, and finished with **Arnt Nettie in AI. Ânt Nettie would be another option,** to pronounce it either way, and not confuse it with an insect. The **option of 'hwiel' for 'while'** was exercised in the BI paragraph (a hold-out from the centuries old whine/wine merge).

Thə nekst igzarmpəlz ov BI and AI wil shoe thə **priemәry stresd vouәl soundz** ov eech werd that iz toò or mor siləbəlz long. **This wil bee shoen bie an әkúet áksәnt on thә ferst leter ov thə moest stresd vouәl sound in thә werd.** This sekshən iz inkloodəd too ferther dəliver on thə promis ov IMS beeing eezyer too prәnouns oever trad Eng. It wil bee inkloodəd in eny IMS Word Listz for Speling, or Dikshәnəryz.

See **(BI)** and **(AI)** on page 12.

This sekshən phroo paij 13 shoez thə stresd vouәlz for werdz ov mor than wun siləbəl. Yoo wil see that **moest werdz ar stresd on thə ferst siləbəl**, meening that wuns wee lern that lesən, wee kan skip this unnesәsәry step, and **simply aksent siləbәlz ov priemәry stres that kum sekәnd, therd, or biyond.** Ә stuedәnt or rieter need not bee obligaetəd too orlwaez maek theez noetaeshәnz, but it wil bee inkurijd in publishd werkz and ree-publishing in IMS, pәtikueləly for nue reederz or ISL (Inglish az ə Sekәnd Laŋwij).

In trad Eng, thə persәnəl proenoun for wunself iz 'I' (kapitәl 'ie'). **In BI, wee keep it fәnetik with 'Ie'** (kapitәl 'ie' + 'e'). **In AI, wee uez thee 'I'** (kapitәl 'i') **and prәnouns it 'ie'**, ə rair eksepshәn too thə spel/proenoe rool.

This tiem wee startəd with thə ***N opshәn for Ant Nettie in BI**, and finishd with **Arnt Nettie in AI. Ânt Nettie wəd bee әnuther opshәn**, too prәnouns it iether wae, and not konfuez it with an insekt. Thee **opshәn ov 'hwiel' for 'while/wiel'** woz eksersiezd in thə BI pa'rәgrarf. (ə hoeld-out from thə senchәryz oeld 'whine/wine' merj)

(Baesik IMS Әbuv. Advâncd IMS Bәloe.)

In trad Eng, thə persәnəl proenoun for wunself iz 'I' (kapitәl 'ie'). **In BI, wee keep it fәnetik with 'Ie'** (kapitәl 'ie' + 'e'). **In AI, wee uez thee 'I'** (kapitәl 'I') **and prәnounc it 'ie'**, ə raer excepshәn too thə spel/proenoe rool.

This tiem wee startəd with thə ***N opshәn for Ant Nettie in BI**, and finishd with **Arnt Nettie in AI. Ânt Nettie wəd bee әnuther opshәn**, too prәnounc it iether way, and not konfuez it with an insekt. Thee **opshәn ov 'hwiel' for 'while/wiel'** woz exerciezd in thə BI pa'rәgrarf (ə hoeld-out from thə cenchәryz oeld 'whine/wine' merj).

Here is one more set of sample paragraphs in Inglish Maed Simpəl, with the mainly stressed syllable of each word also being accented:

(BI) Thair woz noe spaes in thə tíeny kábin for nérvəs páesing. Ə skant aet feet sépəraetəd thə hórlwae éntrəns from thə smorl pórt'hoel, that shoed thə dul blak ov spaes; and əkrós thə dístəns, from thə lokd dor on wun síedworl, too that on thee úther, kəd hav been spand bie thə ɣung man's armz. Oénly hiz iez wer free too roem, and thae wer tíeərd from éndləs repətíshən.

(AI) Thaer woz noe spaec in thə tíeny kábin for nérvəs páecing. Ə skant aet feet sépəraetəd thə háulway éntrənc from thə smaul pórt'hoel, that shoed thə dul blak ov spaec; and əkrós thə distənc, from thə lokd dor on wun síedwaul, too that on thee úther, kəd hav been spand bẏ thə ɣung man'z armz. Oénly hiz ẏz wer free too roam, and thae wer tíeərd from éndləs repətíshən.

Notice the similarities and differences between BI and AI. Words like **space/pacing** become **spaes/paesing** and **spaec/paecing**. The '**k**' must replace the '**c**', if it is a '**k**' sound. A word like **hallway** becomes **horlwae** or **haulway**, finding a closer match to trad Eng in AI. A comprehensive Word List will determine this, possibly as part of a dictionary. The acute accent mark is used on the first vowel of the stressed syllable, like **nérvəs, riskáe, vióelə, bənánə** and **tíeərd**. However, if we cover only words stressed other than on the first syllable, we can ignore the rest.

IMS SOUNDS EXACTLY LIKE TRADITIONAL ENGLISH!

Hopefully the above statement is obvious and redundant to say, but it is important enough to repeat once more to students and first-time viewers of Inglish Maed Simpəl.

Words can be pronounced with the voice, the lips, the tongue, and the teeth. A good dictionary will expound (set forth in detail) on this, and show how sounds like 'thə', 'phree', and many others, are pronounced. **IMS is solely about simplifying the English language to reflect the pronunciation as exactly as possible.** The spelling of some words will change a lot. Others will remain the same.

Don't have an accent? I'm sorry, but that is not possible! It just seems that way if most of what you hear is the same accent as yours. Queen's English, Cockney, a BBC accent (but could be Oxford, Scots from Edinburgh, Yorkshire, Lancashire, southeast England), Boston, California, Texas, New York, Alabama, Ireland, Australia; these are just a few of the many different English accents.

Heer iz wun mor set ov sarmpəl pa'rəgrarfz in Inglish Maed Simpəl with thə maen stresd vouəl sound akséntəd:

See **(BI)** and **(AI)** on paej 13

Noetis thə siməlá'rityz and difrənsəz bətween BI and AI. Werdz liek **space/pacing** bikúm **spaes/paesing** and **spaec/paecing**. Thə **'k'** must rəpláes thə **'c'**, if it iz ə **'k' sound.** Ə werd liek **hallway** bikumz **horlwae** or **haulway**, fiending ə kloeser mach too trad Eng in AI. Ə komprəhénsiv werd list wil ditérmin this, posibly az part ov ə dikshənəry. Thee əkúet aksənt mark iz uezd on thə ferst leter ov thə stresd siləbəl, liek **nérvəs, riskáe, vióelə, banánə,** and **tíeərd.** Houever, if wee kuver oenly werdz stresd uther than on thə ferst siləbəl, wee kan ignor thə rest.

IMS SOUNDZ IGZAKTLY LIEK TRƏDISHƏNƏL INGLISH!

(Baesik IMS Əbúv. Advâncd IMS Bəlóe.)

IMS SOUNDZ IXAKTLY LIEK TRƏDISHƏNƏL INGLISH!

Hoepfəly thee əbúv staetmənt iz obviəs and rədúndənt too say, but it iz importənt inúf too rəpéat wunc mor too stuedəntz and first-tiem vueərz ov Inglish Maed Simpəl.

Werdz kan bee prənóuncd with thə voic, thə lipz, thə tung, and thə teeph. Ə gəd dikshənəry wil expóund (set forph in deetail) on this, and shoe how soundz like 'thə', 'phree', and meny utherz, ar prənóuncd. **IMS iz soely əbout simpləfÿing thee Inglish langwij too riflékt thə prənunciáeshən az exáktly az posibəl.** Thə speling ov sum werdz wil chaenj ə lot. Utherz wil rəmain thə saem.

Doen't hav an aksənt? I'm so'ry, but that iz not posibəl! It just seemz that way if moest ov wot yoo hear iz thə saem aksənt az yorz. Queen'z Inglish, Kokny, ə BBC aksənt (but kəd bee Oxfəd, Skotz from Edinbrə, Yorksher, Lankəsher, soupheast Inglənd), Bostən, Kalifórniə, Texəs, Nue York, Aləbámə, Ierlənd, Ostráeliə; theez ar just ə fue ov thə meny difrənt Inglish aksəntz.

(Shoeing thə prieməry werd stres for IMS other than on thə first siləbəl, iz beeing rizuemd)

MORE On The SCHWA (Ə)

The schwa is the first sound of the soundzəbet ('əh' in IMS). It is the 'a' in **ago,** the 'e' in **silent,** the 'i' in **easily,** the 'o' in **atom,** and the second 'u' in **ruckus.** Its sound has always played a major part in the English language, **being more common than any other vowel sound.** Now the symbol itself will be used in writing English, not just in pronunciation guides.

A backwards, upside down 'e' looks a little like a **printed 'a',** but there are **'a' fonts** that are quite different, along with the most common **written 'a'** also being different. In printed or typed form the 'ə' (əh) has a distinctive straight horizontal line across its middle, like the 'e' (ek) but clearly different. The slight similarity of the 'ə' (əh) to an 'a' is appropriate, since the **unstressed 'uh' (əh)** was represented by the **'a' in trad Eng** more often than by any other letter. **Now that we have 5 sets of symbols for five different 'a' sounds in Baesik IMS (ə, a, ae, air, ar), it is good to have a tried and trusted symbol like the schwa.** In development, a backwards capital 'e' (Ǝ) has been used out of necessity and availability, but **the large rounded version of the smaller schwa is preferred for the capital.**

'FOOT, PUT and WOULD'

Tradition has categorized these words as having a commn vowel sound, sometimes denoted 'oo' in pronunciation keys, and more recently as the **horseshoe 'u'** in the International Phonetic Alphabet (IPA). **Certainly, these three, and many words spelled these ways, have a common vowel sound, but that vowel sound has already been accounted for with the 'uh' (əh) sound of the schwa.** The IPA also uses the **schwa (ə)** for the **'uh' sound** of the 'a' in **about (əbout),** the 'ou' in **furious (fueriəs),** the 'io' of **nation (naeshən),** the 'u' in **circus (serkəs/cirkəs)** or the 'er' in **potter (potə or poter).** Most, if not all, dictionaries seem to be in agreement that the **'uh' (əh) sound,** written **'oo', 'u',** or **'ou',** needs to have a different pronunciation key or symbol to differentiate it from the **'uh' (əh) of alone (əloen), easily (eezəly/eazəly), or abacus (abəkəs).** One definition of the schwa is: **"noun: the usual sound of the vowel in a syllable that is not accented (stressed) at all".** Interestingly, the author could find only a few words of more than one syllable that <u>were</u> stressed on the 'uh' (ə) vowel sound, and these were words of the **'foot, put, would'** variety, such as **afoot, put-on, couldn't** and **wooden.** Giving the **'foot, put, would'** vowel sounds their own vowel, because a very few of them might have two syllables and be stressed, is outside the philosophy of Inglish Maed Simpəl. **To make a case against 200 years of contrary agreement, leave out the vowels of 'foot, put, would'.** So now we have **'ft, pt, wd',** ignoring the silent 'l' (el) of 'could, should or would'. **If you did this correctly, we now have 'fət, pət, wəd', whether we use our vowel of default (ə) or not!**

Also of note, leaving out a second vowel on words like 'simple/simpl' was tried and rejected, because the **schwa, in words like 'simpəl', makes it clear and certain**; it is **'sim-pəl',** not 'sim-plə' or one fat syllable like 'simpl', where you try to swallow the em, pee, and el.

MOR On The SHWAR (Ə)

Thə shwar iz thə ferst sound ov thə soundzəbet (əh in IMS). It iz thee 'a' in **ago**, thee 'e' in **silent**, thee 'i' in **easily**, thee 'o' in **atom**, and thə sekənd 'u' in **ruckus**. (əgoe, sielənt, eezəly, atəm, rukəs) Itz sound haz orlwaez plaed ə maejer part in thə Inglish langwij, **beeing mor komən than eny uther vouəl sound.** Nou thə simbəl itself wil bee uezd in rieting Inglish, not just thə prənunsiáeshən giedz.

Ə bakwədz, upsied doun 'e' ləks ə litəl like ə **printəd 'a'**, but thair ar 'a' fontz that ar qiet difrənt, əlong with thə moest komən **ritən 'a'** orlsoe beeing difrənt. In printəd or tiepd form thee 'ə' (əh) haz ə distínktiv straet ho'rizóntəl lien əkrós itz midəl, like thee 'e' (ek) but kleerly difrənt. Thə sliet similá'rity ov thee 'ə' (əh) too an 'a' iz əpróepriət, sins thee **unstresd 'uh'** (əh) woz reprəzéntəd bie thee 'a' in trad Eng mor ofən than bie eny uther leter. **Nou that wee hav 5 setz ov simbəlz for fiev difrənt 'a' soundz in Baesik IMS (ə, a, ae, air, ar), it iz gəd too hav ə tried and trustəd simbəl like thə shwar.** In dəvéləpmənt, ə bakwədz kapitəl 'e' (Ǝ) haz been uezd out ov nisésity and əvaeləbílity, but **thə larj roundəd vershən ov thə smorler shwar iz prəférd for thə kapitəl.**

'FOOT, PUT and WOULD'

Trədíshən haz katəgəriezd theez werdz az having ə komən vouəl sound, sumtiemz dinóetəd 'oo' in prənunsiáeshən kyz, and mor reesəntly az thə **hors-shoo 'u'** in thee Internáshənəl Fənétik Alfəbet (IPA/IFA). **Sertənly, theez phree, and meny werdz speld theez waez, hav ə komən vouəl sound, but that vouəl sound haz orlrédy been əkóuntəd for with thee 'uh' (əh) sound ov thə shwar.** The IFA orlsoe uezəz thə **shwar (ə)** for thee 'uh' sound ov thee 'a' in **about** (əbóut), thee 'ou' in **furious** (fueriəs), thee 'io' of **nation** (naeshən), thə 'u' in **circus** (serkəs) or thee 'er' in **potter** (potə or poter). Moest, if not orl, dikshənəryz seem too bee in əgréemənt that thee 'uh' (əh) sound, ritən 'oo', 'u', or 'ou', needz too hav ə difərənt prənunsiáeshən ky or simbəl too difərénshiaet it from thee 'uh' (əh) ov **alone** (əlóen), **easily** (eezəly), or **abakus** (abəkəs). Wun definíshən ov thə shwar iz: **"noun: thə uezueəl sound of thə vouəl in ə siləbəl that iz not aksentəd (stresd) at orl"**. Intərestingly, thee orther kəd fiend oenly ə fue werdz ov mor than wun siləbəl that <u>wer</u> stresd on thee 'uh' (ə) vouəl sound, and theez wer werdz ov thə **'foot, put, would'** vəríeəty, such az **afóot, put-on, couldn't** and **wooden.** Giving thə **'foot, put, would'** vouel soundz thair oen vouəl, bikóz ə very fue ov them miet hav toó siləbəlz and bee stresd, iz outsíed thə filósəfy ov Inglish Maed Simpəl. **Too maek ə kaes əgáenst 200 yeerz ov kontrəry əgréemənt, leev out thə vouəlz ov 'foot, put, would'.** Soe nou wee hav **'ft, pt, wd'**, ignóring thə sielənt 'l' (el) ov 'could, should or would'. **If yoo did this kəréktly, wee nou hav 'fət, pət, wəd', wether wee uez our vouəl ov difórlt (ə) or not!**

Orlsoe of noet, leeving out ə sekənd vouəl on werdz like 'simple/simpl' woz tried and rijéktəd, bikóz thə **shwar, in werdz like 'simpəl', maeks it kleer and sertən;** it iz **'sim-pəl'**, not 'simplə' or wun fat siləbəl like 'simpl', where you trie too swoloe thee em, pee and el.

Paej 14a (This paej iz in Baesik Inglish Maed Simpəl) (BI)

IMS has been carefully crafted to maintain the flavour and look of traditional English, especially Advanced IMS. I predict a further evolution, perhaps several decades down the road, when we can shorten all AI's vowel sounds to one letter. But we need a little time to decide if we want to do that, and to first get comfortable using Inglish Maed Simpəl, with a very few symbols that are only slightly different, along with so many that are already familiar. **Those familiar with English are already familiar with more than fifty letters and diphthongs on the AI soundsabet,** plus the many other familiar letter combinations that are too obvious to include on the soundsabet. As an example, **the use of an 'e' to lengthen** other vowels (e.g. **rod** to **rode/roed**) works much better in IMS than it did before in trad Eng.

Accents and Dialects

Accents are something to celebrate, but also to be cautious of, when first learning English. It would not help the Filipino to learn English with a strong Newcastle accent, and expect to use it in New York! At age 9 this author returned with his parents to England, on leave from Africa. **On the London Underground, I listened to my father converse in English with someone I was sure was <u>not</u> speaking English. But this man was Scots, from Glasgow, Scotland and he <u>was</u> speaking English!** In British East Africa, as it was then, my hearing had been limited to only four or five English accents, versus the very many distinctively different accents in Britain and Ireland (about 15), along with another four or five in North America.

Many years later the tables were turned, when I took my American wife for a holiday in Britain and Ireland. **We were having lunch in a Welsh pub, and she listened to me speaking English to a local, that she felt very certain was talking back to me in Welsh!** (the Celtic language of Wales) **Of course, we both spoke English in two very different accents:** his accent being Welsh, and mine from southern England, modified by 15 years in Canada and the USA.

With so many different accents for the same English language, it might be questionable how this works out at all! But it <u>does</u> work out quite well, with <u>your</u> idea of how a word or syllable should sound becoming quite something else, when the other person says it!

But hang in there and <u>listen</u>, knowing the other person <u>is</u> speaking English, and words will come to you, if you are already familiar with English in your own accent. Once you understand most of what is being said, you can ask for a repeat, or different wording, on the tougher words. We already saw the difference between the Northern England *N dialect, where they say 'gras' (IMS) for 'grass' (trad Eng), along with much of North America, versus the Southern England *S accent, where they say 'grars' (IMS) for the same word, along with parts of the northeastern seaboard. Only in this instance, and the duty/beauty issue, was it necessary to have two versions, both easily handled on page 7. **Most of the time, the exact same words will produce a variety of recognisable, but very different sounds, according to the accent.**

IMS haz been kaerfəly krâftəd too maintáin thə flaever and lək ov trədíshənəl Inglish, espéshəly Advâncd IMS. I pridíkt ə further eevəlóoshən, perhapz sevərəl dekaedz down thə road, wen wee kan shortən aul AI'z vowəlz too wun leter. But wee need ə litəl tiem too dicíed if wee wont too doo that, and too first get kumftəbəl uezing Inglish Maed Simpəl, with ə ve'ry fue simbəlz that ar oenly slietly difrənt, əlóng with soe meny that ar aulrédy fəmíliər. **Thoez fəmíliər with Inglish ar aulrédy fəmíliər with mor than fifty leterz and difphongz on thee AI soundzəbet**, plus thə meny uther fəmíliər leter kombináeshənz that ar too obviəs too inklóod on thə soundzəbet. Az an exâmpəl, **thə ues ov an 'e'** too lengthən uther vowəlz (e.g. **rod** too **rode/roed**) werkz much beter in IMS than it did bifór in trad Eng.

Akcentz and Dialectz

Akcentz ar sumphing too celəbraet, but aulsoe too bee caushəs ov, wen first lerning Inglish. It wəd not help thə Filipéenoe too lern Inglish with ə strong Newcastle (nuekâsəl) akcənt, and expékt too uez it in Nue York! At aeg 9 this auther rətúrnd with hiz paerəntz too Inglənd, on leav from Afrikə. **On thə Lundən Underground, I lisənd too mý fâther convérs in Inglish with sumwun I woz shor woz _not_ speaking Inglish. But this man woz Skotz, from Glazgoe, Skotlənd and hee _woz_ speaking Inglish!** In British East Afrikə, az it woz then, mý hearing had been limitəd too oenly fau* or fiev Inglish akcəntz, versəz thə ve'ry meny distínktivly difrənt akcəntz in Britən and Ierlənd (əbout 15), əlong with ənúther 4 or 5 in Norph Əmé'rikə. (*let thə Werd List dicíed on főr, fau or faw, for 'four')

Meny yearz laeter thə taebəlz wer turnd, wen I tək mý Əmé'rikən wief for ə holiday in Britən and Ierlənd. **Wee wer having lunch in ə Welsh pub, and shee lisənd too mee speaking Inglish too ə loekəl, that shee felt ve'ry certən woz tauking bak too mee in Welsh!** (thə Celtik langwij ov Waelz) **Of kors, wee boph spoek Inglish in toó ve'ry difrənt akcəntz:** hiz akcənt beeing Welsh, and mien from suthern Inglənd, modified bý 15 yearz in Kanədə and thə USƏ.

With soe meny difrənt akcəntz for thə saem Inglish langwij, it miet bee qestiənəbəl how this werkz out at aul! But it _duz_ werk out qiet wel, with _yor_ iedíə ov how ə werd or siləbəl shəd sound, bikúming qiet sumphing els, wen thee uther persən sez it!

But hang in thaer and _lisən_, nóeing thee uther persən _iz_ speaking Inglish, and werdz wil kum too yoo, if yoo ar aulrédy fəmíliər with Inglish in yor oen akcənt. Wunc yoo understánd moest ov wot iz beeing sed, yoo kan âsk for ə rəpéat, or diferənt werding, on thə tufer werdz. Wee aulrédy saw thə difrənc bətween thə Northən Inglənd *N dieəlekt, waer thae say 'gras' (IMS) for 'grass' (trad Eng), əlong with much ov Norph Əmé'rikə, versəs thə Suthən Inglənd *S akcənt, waer thay say 'grars' (IMS) for thə saem werd, əlong with partz ov thə norpheastən seabord. Oenly in this instənc, and thə duty/beauty issue, woz it necəsəry too hav toó vershənz, boeph easəly handəld on paej 7. **Moest ov thə tiem, thee ixakt saem werdz wil prəjoos ə vəríeəty ov rekogniesəbəl, but ve'ry difrənt soundz, əkórding too thee akcənt.**

Paej 15a (This paej iz in Advâncd Inglish Maed Simpəl) (AI)

A somewhat divergent accent, meaning sounds have not only been changed, but the variety of sounds has also been diminished, may produce a further liability, if it then teaches others. To some degree this has occurred with the United States teaching English to what was their only full-size colony, the Philippines (independent since 1945) and a few other bases around the world. The result is almost as hard to untangle as the Glasgow accent. Closely related to this, **recent copies of the Webster New World Dictionary © are missing three vowel sounds in the pronunciation guide, that have traditionally been included in the English language.** In balance, one should also acknowledge that America produced the prolific Noah Webster, pioneer of Written English, Spelling, and some of the earliest and most complete English Dictionaries.

The writer's adopted country, Canada, deserves similar criticism for its more or less homogenized accent, described by Oxford's Canadian Dictionary © as treating **'Mary, merry, marry'** as practically the same sound. But check the soundsabets and you will see: **Maery/ Mairy (aer/air), me'ry (e), ma'ry (a). These are three distinctly different sounds!** They are being preserved and used by accents that <u>do</u> treat them differently, and especially by IMS itself.

Also, there is no perfect person to introduce IMS. You are stuck with someone born in southern England, educated in British East Africa and England, naturalized in Canada, and residenced in the USA and Canada. **Prefer to put it to a committee of professors and writers from a prestigious English speaking university?** It could come to that, perhaps; meanwhile, the only way to <u>get</u> <u>started</u> is how most things get started, by **a single individual with a workable plan.**

Correctly spelling words according to their pronunciation, followed by very simple unwavering rules, is a first step to slow down or arrest the tendency for the language to lose its variety and clarity of sounds.

Let us say that the IMS sound **'a'** (alphabet letter **'ak'**) degenerates to the **'ə'** sound **(əh)** in several common words; or the **'e'** sound **(ek)** devolves to the **'i' (ik)**, or perhaps all the way to the **'ə'**. Or a word like **'magic' (majik)** slips to **mujək, məjək** or **məzjək** in a key or broadly used dialect. Then the primary English dictionary producers, assisted or not by a prestigious group of writers and professors, might agree among themselves to retain the earlier, more definitive sounds, by simply leaving that pronunciation and spelling there, alongside the somewhat degenerated prono/spelling, and labelling the latter as a slang or informal entry, if that is what it has become. **Thus the original or earlier, more vibrant and differentiating sounds would minimumly be retained for <u>formal</u> speech and writing, and may also return to <u>normal</u> speech and writing.**

Ə sumwot dievérjənt aksənt, meening soundz hav not oenly been chaenjd, but thə vəríeəty ov soundz haz orlsoe been dimínishd, mae prədúes ə ferther lieəbíləty, if it then teechəz utherz. Too sum dəgree this haz əkérd with thee Ueníetəd Staetz teeching Inglish too wot woz thair oenly fəl-siez kolony, thə Filipéenz (indipéndənt sins 1945) and ə fue uther baesəz əround thə werld. Thə rizúlt iz orlmoest az hard too untángəl az the Glazgoe aksənt. Kloesly rəláetəd too this, **reesənt kopyz* ov thə Webster Nue World Dikshənəry © ar mising phree vouəl soundz in thə prənunsiáeshən gied, that hav trədíshənəly been inklóodəd in thee Inglish langwij.** In baləns, wun shəd orlsoe aknólij that Əmé'rikə prədúesd thə prəlífik Noeəh Webster, pieəníər ov Ritən Inglish, Speling, and sum ov thee erliəst and moest kəmpléet Inglish Dikshənəryz*. (*noet ues ov shorter 'y' instead ov 'ee')

Thə rieter'z ədóptəd kunchry, Kanədə, dizérvz similer kritisizəm for itz mor or les həmójəniezd aksənt, diskríebd bie Oksfəd'z Kənáediən Dikshənəry © az treeting **'Mary, merry, mary'** az praktikəly thə saem sound. But chek thə soundzəbetz and yoo wil see: **"Maery/Mairy (aer/air), me'ry (ə), ma'ry (a). Theez ar phree distínktly difrənt soundz!** Thae ar beeing prəzérvd and uezd bie aksəntz that doo treet them difrəntly, and espéshəly bie IMS itself.

Orlsoe, thair iz noe perfekt persən too intrədúes IMS. Yoo ar stuk with sumwun born in suthən Ingländ, eduekaetəd in British Eest Afrikə and Ingländ, natuerəliezd in Kanədə, and rezidənsd in thə USƏ and Kanədə. **Prəfér too pət it too ə komítee ov prəféserz and rieterz from ə prəstíjəs Inglish speeking uenivérsity?** It kəd kum too that, perhápz; meenwiel, thee oenly wae too get startəd iz hou moest phingz get startəd, by ə singəl indivídueəl with ə werkəbəl plan.

Kəréktly speling werdz əkórding too thair prənunsiáeshən, foloed bie very simpəl unwáevering roolz, iz ə ferst step too sloe doun or ərést thə tendənsy for thə langwij too looz itz vəríeəty and kla'rity ov soundz.

Let us say that thee IMS sound 'a' (alfəbet leter 'ak') digénəraetz too thee 'ə' sound (əh) in sevərəl komən werdz; or thee 'e' sound (ek) dəvolves too the 'i' (ik), or perhápz orl thə wae too thə 'ə' (əh). Or ə werd like **'magic'** (majik) slipz too **mujək, məjək** or **məzjək** in ə kee or brordly uezd dieəlekt. Then thə priem

əry Inglish dikshənəry prədúeserz, əsístəd or not bie ə prestíjəs groop ov rieterz and prəféserz, miet əgree əmúng themselvz to ritáen thee erlier, mor difínitiv soundz, bie simply leeving that prənunsiáeshən and speling thair, əlóngsied thə sumwot dijénəraetəd proenoe/speling, and laebəling thə later az ə slang or infórməl entry, if that iz wot it haz bikum. **Thus thee əríjinəl or erlier, mor viebrənt and diferénshiaeting soundz wəd miniməmly bee ritáend for forməl speech and rieting, and mae orlsoe ritérn too norməl speech and rieting.**

We have not been used to English spelling exactly defining the way the word is pronounced. With IMS, that is exactly what we have, especially in the most common dialects. Once we move into the colonisation of the solar system and outer space, whatever we call it and however we do it, such a safeguard to the continued clarity of our already international language should prove invaluable to future generations, in the vast distances, time lags and isolations of space. Compare the distance and time taken to travel between London to Liverpool to Glasgow (three wildly different accents, but not far apart), on to Jupiter's moon, Europa, and then to Alpha Centauri, our nearest star system, four light years away.

For hundreds of years now, there has been a desire to sort out the spelling of the English language. William Caxton brought the printing press to London in 1476, at which time spelling became important, but poorly served by foreign ideas and poorly translated English bibles in the following century. Even Caxton, an English merchant, had spent more time in Europe and had a poor command of the written language. Typesetters, paid by the line, developed an understandable taste for long words. **But we can fix it now! And Inglish Maed Simpəl will in no way invalidate the evolving free spirited nature of the English language!**

Derivations and History of Words will continue to be included in good dictionaries, so don't think that 'no nonsense' spelling will obscure this. While a little more needs to be said about the spelling of the original word, **the pronunciation will be right there, in the spelling!** Some words we prefer to pronounce in a foreign tongue; we can still do this, and follow the word in the text with a bracketed IMS transliteration, as indicated for proper nouns earlier (page 11).

IMS BECOMES THE STANDARD METHOD OF WRITING ENGLISH

First and Second Language English Speakers Prefer to Read and Write with Inglish Maed Simpəl

Any successful project, creation or invention has an Ideal Scene, like the two above, that the project manager, creator or inventor strives to obtain. These ideal scenes are real and predictable, because the student only has to understand and apply this short IMS Manual, to be able to read and pronounce anything in Inglish Maed Simpəl. Conversely, a knowledge of the BI soundsabet and its 43 symbols, based on an expanded ABC alphabet, permits any student to write and correctly spell what he hears. While a knowledge of Advanced IMS requires knowing close to 60 symbols, also based on the ABC alphabet, its similarity to trad Eng makes it a simple task for current English speakers, and still not a difficult learn for new students, who can celebrate the relative simplicity of English spelling from now on.

Wee hav not been uezd too Inglish speling ixáktly difíening thə way thə werd iz prənóuncd. With IMS, that iz ixáktly wot wee hav, espéshəly in thə moest komən dieəlektz. Wunc wee moov intoo thə koləniezáeshən ov thə soeler sistəm and outer spaec, wotéver wee kaul it and howéver wee doo it, such ə saefgard too thə kontínued kla'rity ov our aulrédy internáshənəl langwij shəd proov inválueəbəl too fuecher jenəráeshənz, in thə vâst distəncəs, tiem lagz and iesəláeshənz ov spaec. Kompáer thə distənc and tiem taekən too travəl bətween Lundən too Liverpool too Glazgoe (phree wieldly difrənt akcəntz, but not far əpart), on too Joopiter'z moon, Ueróepə, and then too Alfə Centáury, our nearəst star sistəm, fau liet yearz əway.

For hundrədz ov yearz now, thaer haz been ə dəzíer too sort out thə speling ov thee Inglish langwij. Wiliəm Kaxtən braut thə printing pres too Lundən in 1476, at wich tiem speling bikáem importənt, but porly servd bẏ fo'rin iedyəz and porly translaetəd Inglish biebəlz in thə foloeing cenchəry. Eevən Kaxtən, an Inglish merchənt, had spent mor tiem in Uerəp, and had ə por kəmând ov thə ritən langwij. Tẏpseterz, paid bẏ thə lien, dəvéləpd an understándəbəl taest for long werdz. **But wee kan fix it now! And Inglish Maed Simpəl wil in noe way inválədaet thee ivólving free spi'ritəd naecher ov thee Inglish langwij!**

De'riváeshənz and History ov Werdz wil kontínue too bee inkloodəd in gəd dikshənəryz, soe doen't phink that 'noe nonsenc' speling wil obskúer this. Wiel ə litəl mor needz too bee sed əbout thee o'ríjinəl werd (speling histəry), **the pronunciáeshən wil be riet thaer, in thə speling!** Some werdz wee prəfer too prənóunc in ə fo'rin tung; we kan stil doo this, and foloe thə werd in thə text with ə brakitəd IMS trazlítəraeshən, az indikáetəd for proper nounz erlyer (paej 11).

IMS BIKUMZ THƏ STANDERD METHƏD OV RIETING INGLISH

First and Sekənd Langwij Inglish Speakerz Prəfér too Read and Riet with Inglish Maed Simpəl

Any sukcésfəl projekt, kriáeshən or invénshən haz an Iedeal Sean*, like thə toó əbúv, that thə projekt manəjer, kriáeter or invénter strievz too obtáin. (*sean for 'scene' az seen taekən) Theez iedeal seanz ar real and prədíktəbəl, bikóz thə stuedənt oenly haz too understánd and əplẏ this short IMS Manueəl, too bee aebəl too read and prənóunc enyphing in Inglish Maed Simpəl. Konvérsly, ə nolij ov thə BI soundzəbet and itz 43 simbəlz, baesd on an expándəd ABC alfəbet, permítz eny stuedənt too riet and kəréktly spel wot he hearz. Wiel ə nolij ov Advâncd IMS riqíearz noeing kloes too 60 simbəlz, aulsoe baesd on an expándəd ABC alfəbet, its similá'rity too trad Eng maekz it ə simpəl tâsk for ku'rənt Inglish speakerz, and stil not ə difikəlt lern for nue stuedəntz, hoo kan celəbraet thə relətiv simplícity ov Inglish speling from now on.

Paej 17a (This paej iz in Advâncd Inglish Maed Simpəl) (AI)

CONCLUSION

As we move rapidly into the Computer and Internet Age, and more slowly into the Space Age, the human race needs an International language, and appears to have chosen English. Inglish Maed Simpəl will make it easier to learn and remember for everyone. Those whose first language used an alphabet different from the Roman (ABC), as is the case of many Asian, Middle East and Eastern European countries, will now find the learning a lot easier, and the understanding much better, with IMS. And **understanding is,** after all, **the primary purpose of a language.**

Soon we will count English speakers in multiple billions, and, shortly after that, export it to other planets. That is, if we can keep this one long enough…. We have such a beautiful planet here, but Earth is also an anarchy of selfish, bickering nations, many of whose leaders and citizens would gamble it all away for money, power, superstition, or unreasoning hate and anger. With world-destroying nuclear missiles in many arsenals, and so many countries still thinking that war and military force are viable options, it's perhaps a wonder we have made it to 2020. On top of all this, or because of it, our oceans are 90% depleted of fish and sea life on a predominantly water planet.

Even so, there is reason to hope to get through all this. We hear only the bad in the 'news', but technology to resolve the social problems of the human race has been making its way into society since 1950, if you are smart enough to find it. We came very close to radiating Earth beyond a point of no return mid 20th century. Getting all on board for the Test Ban Treaty occurred only in the nick of time. Many of our leaders and governments are too pathetic to be left to their own devices, but some countries have transformed and earned our respect, such as 21st century Germany. We are seeing some steps in the right direction from a lot of countries and organizations, including New Zealand and Canada. And let's not forget to acknowledge that world hunger is greatly reduced and lifespans greatly increased, compared to a few decades ago. **So, if we can just hold the planet together, this English language will have no problem surviving and flourishing for another thousand, or ten thousand years. And especially now that we have Inglish Maed Simpəl!**

By the way, this Manual and IMS have been prepared in Canada and the USA, with the author born and educated in the UK and British East Africa; Canadian and British spelling has extra 'u's and double consonants, like the double 'l' (el), compared to the USA. **So don't worry if the trad Eng spelling is this way or that: in IMS it will be exactly as it is in this manual: sensible, logical, easy to read, easy to pronounce, easy to write, and,** once you make the initial effort, **easy to understand.**

KONKLOOZJƏN

Az wee moov rapidly intoo thə Kompúeter and Internet Aej, and mor sloely intoo thə Spaes Aej, thə huemən raes needz an Internáshənəl langwij, and əpeerz too hav choezən Inglish. Inglish Maed Simpəl wil maek it eezier too lern and rimémber for evrywun. Thoez hooz ferst langwij uezd an alfəbet difrənt from thə Roemən (ABC), az in thə kaes ov meny Aezjən, Midəl Eest, and Eestern Uerəpíən Kunchryz, wil nou fiend thə lerning ə lot eezyer, and thee understánding much beter, with IMS. And **understánding iz,** âfter orl, **thə prieməry perpəs ov ə langwij.**

Soon wee wil kount Inglish speekerz in multipəl biliənz, and shortly âfter that, eksport it too uther planitz. That iz, if wee kan keep this wun long inúf…. Wee hav such ə buetifəl planit heer, but Erph iz orlsoe an anarky ov selfish, bikering naeshənz, meny ov hooz leederz and sitizənz wəd gambəl it orl əwáe for muny, pouər, sooperstíshən, or unréezəning haet and anger. With world-distróiing nueklier misielz in meny arsənəlz, and soe meny kunchryz stil phinking that wor and militəry fors ar vieəbəl opshənz, it'z perhápz ə wunder that wee hav maed it too 2020. On top ov orl this, or bikóz ov it, our oeshənz ar nienty persént dipléetəd ov fish and seė lief in ə prədóminəntly worter* planit. (*opshənz: woter, worter, wôter)

Eevən soe, thair iz reezən too hoep too get phroo orl this. Wee heer oenly thə bad in thə 'nuez', but teknóləjy too rizólv thə soeshəl probləmz ov thə huemən raes haz been maeking itz wae intoo səsíeəty sins 1950, if yoo ar smart inúf too fiend it. Wee kaem ve'ry kloes too raediaeting Erph biɣónd ə point ov noe ritérn mid twentyiph senchəry. Geting orl on bord for thə Test Ban Treety əkérd oenly in thə nik ov tiem. Meny ov our leederz and guvənməntz ar too pəphétik too bee left too thair oen divíesəz, but sum kunchryz hav transfórmd and ernd our rispékt, such az 21st senchəry Germəny. Wee ar seeing sum stepz in thə riet die'rékshən from ə lot ov kunchryz and orgəniezáeshənz, inklooding Nue Zeelənd and Kanədə. And let'z not forget too aknólij that world hunger iz graetly ridúesd and liefspanz graetly inkréesd, kəmpáird too ə fue dekaedz əgóe. **Soe, if wee kan just hoeld thə planit təgéther, this Inglish langwij wil hav noe probləm servíeving and flurishing for ənuther phouzənd, or ten phousənd yeerz. And espéshəly nou that wee hav Inglish Maed Simpəl!**

Bie thə wae, this Manueəl and IMS hav been prəpáird in Kanədə and thə USƏ, with thə orther born and eduekaetəd in thə UK and British Eest Afrikə; Kənaediən and British speling haz ekstrə 'u'z and dubəl konsənəntz, like thə dubəl 'l' (el), kəmpáird too thə USƏ. **Soe doen't wury if thə trad Eng speling iz this wae or that; in IMS it wil bee igzáktly az it iz in this manueəl: sensibəl, lojikəl, eezy too reed, eezy too prənóuns, eezy too riet, and,** wuns yoo maek thee inishəl efert, **eezy too understánd.**

Paej 18a (This paej in in Baesik Inglish Maed Simpəl) (BI)

Baesik IMS Soundzəbet as it corresponds to the IPA/IFA

Take another look at this chart and see where IMS fits in with the International Phonetic Alphabet. We adopt the regular schwa, but not the smaller modifier shown in some dictionaries.

Ə　ə ......bək, əlóu, serkəs, pət, bundəl.......　ə ᵊ (bundᵊl)

A　a ......hat, ant, malis, gras, at, hapy.....　æ

　　ae .....haet, laezy, fael, kriáeshən, pael....　eɪ

　　air ....fairy, tairing, stair, kəmpáir, air....　ɛə

　　ar ....hart, grars, farther, marvələs......　ɑ: (marvᵊləs)

B　b ....bee, biebəl, əbílity, babəl, briebd.....　(b)

Ch　ch ......cherch, much, chiemz, reech.....　tʃ

D　d ......didúkshən, deer, heed, landəd......　(d)

E　e ......net, entry, egzit, eksit, leter, sel.....　ɛ

　　ee ....leed, eevən, wee, seesied, eeger......　i:

　　er ......herd, fern, merder, prəvíeder........　ɜ:

F　f ....difphong, frendly, of, fortitued, if......　(f)

G　g .....gigəbiet, bagd, graet, biger, gon.......　g

H　h ....bihóeld, heks, unhápiər, houéver.....　(h)

I　i....phinking, hit, skwirəl, pity, riezing.....　ɪ

　　ie...fieər, inkwíer, ieskreem, iedəl.........　aɪ/əɪ

J　j ......jujmənt, jenəráeshən, majikəl......　dʒ

K　k ....aktívəty, kərés, kingdəm, fakt........　(k)

L　l ......əlótəd, lily, orlwaez, əlért, luky.......　(l)

M　m .....minsd, moeshən, tram, implíed......　(m)

N　n ...granəry, nuezpaeper, never, nienty...　(n)

　　ng/ŋ ...Iŋlənd, fling, dung, baŋ, phrong.......　ŋ

This chart is an extra check on how to pronounce a particular word. Refer to it as needed when using the soundsabets on pages 3 and four. In IMS we tend to use 'er' in some places where a dictionary might suggest a schwa, to keep the look and flavour of the English language. The difference in pronunciation is minor.

BI to IPA options continued

O	**o** ......job, oliv, prong, pop, ontoo, tol.......		ɒ
	oe .....oepəning, boest, loenly, roed, soe.....		əʊ
	oi ......perlóin, join, kolóidəl, oister, oil......		ɔɪ
	oo ......rooster, troo, roofing, pool, skool....		u:
	or ......ədórn, storyz, ortum, hortikultuer...		ɔ:
P	**p** ...piepz, apəl, printing, impáel, pomp...		(p)
	ph .....phe'rəpy, pheesis, maphəmátiks......		θ
R	**r** ......ma'ryd, travəl, bred, so'ry, ho'rid...		(r)
S	**s** ......səsínktly, klâs, stop, mâst, kis........		(s)
	sh .....shie, shaloe, mashd, British, splash....		ʃ
T	**t** ......triesikəl, ətak, artíkuelaet, testəd		(t)
	th ......râther, thair, uther, muther, this.....		ð
U	**u** ......lukləs, tunəl, Sundae, klub, gulibəl....		ʌ
V	**v** ......viváeshəs, living, striev, vanity........		(v)
W	**w** .....wiet, wiez, orlwaez, wen, əwáir........		(w)
Ɏ	**ɣ** ......bəɣónd, ɣel, ɣestədae, ɣorn, ɣes........		j
Z	**z** ......windz, pleezing, zeebrə, kopyz.........		(z)
	zj ......lezjer, Aezjə, dae zjə vóo, trezjəry......		ʒ

The ABC letters in brackets are used as in the English alphabet. Others have their own interpretation in **IMS (left)** or **IPA (right)**. The English words in the middle are in BI, but be sure you pick the right syllable for the right sound. (e.g. **'riezing'** showcases the **'i'** [ik] in **'ing'**, not the **'ie'** in **'riez'**) As the **'j'** is common in English, it is retained. In IMS the **'y'** is the **vowel** sound **'ee'** for **'aly'**; **'ɣ'** is the consonant for **'yeloe'**. We roll back the **'j'** to **'zj'** for **'plezjer'**. Use of the **'ing'** symbol ŋ is optional. In addition to the **spacer ('), acute accent (á), caret (^) and dotter (ė)**, the **reverse !/? (¡¿)** is also recommended for the **IMS keyboard**, along with Ə ə, Ɏ ɣ, ŋ and a larger full stop. There are practically no truly English words starting with an 'x', but 'ex' is quite common; **BI** nails it with **eks** or **igz**, which can be written as **'ex'** or **'ix'** in **AI**. The recent insanity of presenting more Chinese words starting with an **X** will be tempered by IMS; if a 'new' sound like **'Shee'** for **Xi** is wanted, it will need to start with **'sh'**. You can use this chart for AI-to-IPA options also.

IMS Afterword and Numbers Simplified (Refer to NS tables starting page 22)

Inglish Maed Simpəl was first completed, minus editing and further improvements, on the last day of 2015. It was very significant that this led <u>immediately</u> to a **new system of naming and representing our Hindu/Arab numbers,** devised the very next day on the 1ˢᵗ of January 2016. **This inovation will probably not interest everyone at first, but the fact that the simplicity of IMS led to the shortest spoken numerical system, based on the English language, which has up until now had a most cumbersome, plodding numerical language, is really quite astounding!** Naturally, this fact validates Inglish Maed Simpəl; highly workable inovations will beget other highly workable inovations.

It still took a few more years to get the book to print, with many improvements and refinements that will hopefully make the wait worthwhile. **Transliterating* texts and existing books is the best way to show the benefits of IMS, so this will be the next step, after introducing the manual.** Meanwhile, hunkering down against the Covid-19 pandemic in the spring of 2020, your author hopes to explain **a new way to represent our numbers from 0 to 9, and then on up through tens, hundreds, thousands, millions, up to 10 to the power of 30** (currently one nonillion in the US system), **and all based on these IMS sounds.** (*write a letter or word using the closest corresponding letters of a different alphabet)

Numbers Simplified (NS) was inspired by a friend's comment on the simplicity of words for numbers in the Far East, compared to ours in English. **Besides a simpler, more logical ten digits, 0 to 9 borrows ten hard vowels from the IMS soundsabet: oi, ae, ee, ie, oe, oo, ar, er, or, ou.** These short syllables do not even have a consonant until 10 is reached. Then **ten, twenty, thirty** and so on, are voiced with a single consonant after the letter/sound 'o' (as in 'hot'), as follows: **ob, og, oj, ok, ol, on, op, oɣə, oz,** and then **och** for a **hundred.** (oɣə uses 'ɣ' {ɣae}; avoid confusion with 'oi/oy') A **thousand** is next. We use the **M** for **mille**, 1000 in Latin, as **om.** Voiced, any number in NS is very much **shorter to say than in English and a lot shorter than in Korean, which is the shortest up until now.**

After ten you simply add the double digit vowel to the single digit consonant, as **ob, bae, bee, bie, boe, boo, bar, ber, bor,bou, og, gae, gee, gie,** and so on. This applies equally to the rest of the tens, through 90, as seen in the first chart. You might notice that a lot of symbols are in **alphabetical order, like 1-5, 6-9 and the tens (B-Z),** which assists learning and memory for many of us. For multiple **hundreds,** simply add **ee, ie, oe, oo, etc.** in front of the consonant **(eech, iech, oech, ooch).** Do the same with **thousands (eem, iem, oem, oom)** all the way up to **osh** (thirty zeroes or 10^{30}), as **eesh, iesh, oesh, oosh,** and so on.

IMS Âfterwerd and Numberz Simplified (Rəfer too NS taebəlz starting paej 22)

Inglish Maed Simpəl woz first kəmpléetəd, mienəs editing and further impróovməntz, on thə lâst day ov 2015. It woz ve'ry signífikənt that this led <u>iméediətly</u> too ə **nue sistəm ov naeming and reprəzénting our Hindoo/A'rəb numberz**, dəvíezd thə ve'ry next day on thə 1ˢᵗ ov Janueəry 2016. **This inəváeshən wil probəbly not interest every wun at first, but thə fakt that thə simplícity ov IMS led too thə shortəst spoekən nuemé'rikəl sistəm, baesd on thee Inglish langwij, wich haz up until now had ə moest cumbersəm, ploding nuemé'rikəl langwij, iz realy qiet astóunding!** Natuerəly, this fakt validaetz Inglish Maed Simpəl; hiely werkəbəl inəváeshənz wil bigét uther hiely werkəbəl inəváeshənz.

It stil tək ə fue mor yearz too get thə bək too print, with meny impróovməntz and rəfíenməntz that wil hoepfəly maek thə wait werphwíel. **Tranzlíteraeting* textz and exísting bəkz iz thə best way too shoe thə benəfitz ov IMS, soe this wil bee thə next step, âfter intrədúecing thə manueəl.** Meanwiel, hunkering down əgainst thə Koevid-19 pandémik in thə spring ov 2020, yor aupher hoepz too explain **ə nue way too reprəzént our numberz from 0 too 9, and then on up phroo tenz, hundrədz, phousəndz, miliənz, up too 10 too thə power ov 30** (cu'rəntly wun noníliən in thə US sistəm), **and aul baesd on theez IMS soundz.** (*riet ə leter or werd uezing thə kloesəst ko'rəsponding leterz ov ə difrənt alfəbet)

Numberz Simplified woz inspierd bẏ ə frend'z komənt on thə simplícity ov werdz for numberz in thə Far East, kəmpáerd too ourz in Inglish. **Bəsíedz ə simpler, mor lojikəl ten dijitz, 0 too 9 bo'roez ten hard vowəlz from thee IMS soundzəbet: oi, ae, ee, ie, oe, oo, ar, er, or, ou.** Theez short siləbəlz doo not eevən hav ə konsənənt until 10 iz reachd. Then **ten, twenty, thirty** and soe on, ar voicd with ə singəl konsənənt âfter thə leter/sound **'o'** (az in **'hot'**), az foloez: **ob, og, oj, ok, ol, on, op, oɣə, oz,** and then **och** for ə **hundrəd**. (**oɣə** uezəz **'ɣ'** {ɣae}; əvoid kənfúezjən with **'oi/oy'**) Ə **phousənd** iz next. Wee uez thee **M** for **mille**, 1000 in Latin, az **om. Voicd, eny number in NS iz ve'ry much shorter too say than in Inglish and a lot shorter than in Ko'ríən, wich iz thə shortəst up until now.**

Âfter ten yoo simply ad thə dubəl dijit vowəl too thə singəl dijit konsənənt, az **ob, bae bee, bie, boe, boo, bar, ber, bor, bou, og, gae, gee, gie,** and soe on. This əpliez eeqəly too thə rest ov thə tenz, phroo 90, az seen in thə first chart. Yoo miet noetic that ə lot ov simbəlz ar in **alfəbétikəl order, like 1-5, 6-9 and thə tenz (B-Z),** wich əsístz lerning and meməry for meny ov us. For multipəl **hundrədz,** simply ad **ee, ie, oe, oo,** etc. in frunt ov thə konsənənt (**eech, iech, oech, ooch**). Doo thə saem with **phousəndz (eem, iem, oem, oom)** aul thə way up too **osh** (thirty zeroez or 10³⁰), az **eesh, iesh, oesh, oosh,** and soe on.

Note that you don't have to put 'ae' (one) in front; it is obviously ae/one hundred, thousand, million, etc. Note also the use of 'o' as a facilitating vowel. It might seem to represent a zero or one, but that is not what it is. It is used in front of a consonant, representing anything from ob (ten) to osh (nonillion, 10 x 3 zeroes, which logically should have been called a decillion). This 'o' (ok) is #23 on the soundsabet in Basic IMS, not #24, 'oe'.

When writing down long numbers, it is expected to make sensible breaks, forming two, three or more words. **Of course, one uses number symbols when writing or typing large numbers, most of the time, but everyone learning this system needs to practice in writing, with letters and words.** If you can **write** it correctly, you will be able to **say** it correctly.

The numbers **0 – 9 (oi-ou)** in NS, or IMS if you prefer, use the symbol **0 (oi)** for zero, and the symbol **8 (oo)** for the middle number (currently 5). **Number symbols 3, 6, 9 continue as themselves, and also as mirror images of themselves to replace 4, 7, and 8.** The new 1 and 2 symbols have taken a little longer to nail down, but using the **Arial font for 1**, and the **backwards 7 for two** (similar to the current Arabic symbol for two/ee) works quite well. **1 (ae)** in this font has a medium sized left-turning barb at the top of a vertical line, and angled down at 45 degrees. The ⌐ (ee) should be straight like its almost mirror-image twin **(1)**. (the Calibri font for 7 works well) The switch from the English 5 to IMS 8 (oo) is acknowledged as a potential short-term confusion. However, **the chance to make the best selection of number symbols is now**, and the classic symbol **8 (oo)** is the very best fit midway between **1 (ae)** and **9 (ou)**. So we end up with: **1, ⌐, 3, Ɛ, 8, 6, ∂, ℓ, 9, 10.**

The old British system of a billion being a million million is being replaced in international use by the American system, that France used to use also, where **each new '-illion' is times one thousand (x1000). NS will keep this more useful system, but correct a few irregularities,** like a thousand now being represented by the **M** of **'mille'**, and the **-illions** having a prefix, or really just a consonant letter or diphthong, relating to **how many sets of three zeros it has, in Latin or English*.** We then have **D** for **duo**, **T** for **three**, **F** for **four**, **Q** for **quinque**, **S** for **six/sext**. Beyond that, the choices diminish and a different sound that works, becomes more important than any other justification: **OV** for **seven** 000s; **OST** for **eight** 000s; **OLK** switches to **KL** for **nine** sets of 000; we end, for now, with **ten** sets of 000 using **SH** as in **osh, eesh, oosh,** etc. (*calling ten sets of 000 a nonillion illustrates this flaw)

Not having got involved so much with mathematics in the current lifetime, and now surpassing 70, the final choices might be left to mathematicians, once they understand the concept. Set at the end of the IMS manual, there may or may not be a high degree of interest in the **fastest spoken 0 (zero/oi) to 9 (nine/ou) number system,** but keeping this a secret would be a disservice to those who can use it, as well as science in general. Be advised, however, that **Inglish Maed Simpəl itself is a completed work ready for use,** with or without Numbers Simplified.

Noet that yoo doen't hav too pət 'ae' (wun) in frunt; it iz obviəsly ae/wun hundrəd, phousənd, miliən, ets. Noet orlsoe thə ues ov 'o' az ə fəsílitaeting vouəl. It miet seem too reprəzént ə zeeroe or wun, but that iz not wot it iz. It iz uezd in frunt ov ə konsənənt, reprəzénting enyphing from **ob (ten)** too **osh (noníliən,** 10 x 3 zeeroez, wich lojikəly shəd hav been korld ə **desíliən).** This **'o' (ok)** iz #23 on thə soundzəbet in Baesik IMS, not #24, 'oe'.

Wen rieting doun long numberz, it iz ekspéktəd too maek sensibəl braekz, forming toȯ, phree or mor werdz. **Ov kors, wun uezəz number simbəlz wen rieting or tieping larj numberz, moest ov thə tiem, but evrywun lerning this sistəm needz too praktis in rieting, with leterz and werdz.** If yoo kan **riet** it kəréktly, yoo wil bee aebəl too **sae** it kəréktly.

Thə numberz **0 - 9 (oi-ou)** in NS, or IMS if yoo prəfer, uez thə simbəl **0 (oi)** for zero, and thə simbəl **8 (oo)** for thə midəl number (cu'rəntly 5). **Number simbəlz 3, 6, 9 kontínue az themsélvz, and orlsoe az mirer imijəz ov themsélvz, too rəpláes 4, 7, and 8.** Thə nue 1 and 2 simbəlz hav taekən ə litəl longer too nael doun, but uezing thee **Airiəl font for 1,** and thə **bakwədz 7 for toȯ** (siməler too thə kurənt A'rəbik simbəl for toȯ/ee) werkz kwiet wel. **1 (ae)** in this font haz ə meediəm siezd left-terning barb at thə top ov ə vertikəl lien, and angəld doun at 45 dəgreez. Thə Γ **(ee)** shəd bee straet, liek its orlmoest mirer imij twin **(1).** (thə Kaléebry font for 7 werkz wel) Thə swich from thee Inglish 5 too IMS 8 (oo) iz aknólijd az a pəténshəl short-term konfúezjən. Houéver, **thə châns too maek thə best səlékshən ov number simbəlz iz nou,** and thə klasik simbəl **8 (oo)** iz thə ve'ry best fit midwae bətwéen **1 (ae)** and **9 (ou).** Soe wee end up with: **1, Γ, 3, Ɛ, 8, 6, ϑ, Ϥ, 9, 10.**

Thee oeld British sistəm ov ə biliən beeing ə miliən miliən iz beeing ripláesd in internáshənəl uez bie thee Əmé'rikən sistəm that Frâns uezd too uez orlsoe, wair **eech nue '-iliən' iz tiemz wun phouzənd (x1000). NS wil keep this mor uezfəl sistəm, but kərékt ə fue ireguelá'rityz,** like ə phouzənd nou beeing reprəzéntəd bie thee **M** ov 'mille' (meel), and thee **-iliəns** having ə preefikz, or reely just ə konsənənt leter or difphong, rəláeting too **hou meny setz ov phree zeeroez it haz, in Latin or Inglish*.** Wee then hav **D for 'duo'** (dueoe), **T for 'three'** (phree), **F for 'four'** (fȯr), **Q/kw for 'quinque'** (kwinkwae), **S for 'sext/six'** (sekst/siks). Biɣónd that, thə choisəz dimínish and ə diferənt sound that werks, bikúmz mor impórtənt than eny uther justifikáeshən: **OV** for **sevən** 000s; **OST** for **aèt** 000s; **OLK** swichəz too **KL** for **nien** setz ov 000. Wee end, for nou, with **ten** setz ov 000 uezing **SH** az in **osh, eesh, oosh,** ets. (*korling ten setz ov 000 ə 'noníllon' iləstraetz this flor)

Not having got invólved soe much in maphəmátikz in thə kurənt lieftiem, and nou serpâsing 70, this orpher miet leev sum ov thə fienəl choisəz too maphəmatíshənz, wuns thae understánd thə konsept. Set at thee end ov thee IMS manueəl, thair mae or mae not bee ə hie dəgrée ov interest in **thə fâstəst spoekən 0 (oi) too 9 (ou) number sistəm in the world,** but keeping this ə seekrət wəd bee ə dissérvis too thoez hoo kan uez it, az wel az sieəns in jenərəl. Bee advíezd, houéver, that **Inglish Maed Simpəl itself iz ə kəmpléetəd werk redy for ues,** with or withóut Numberz Simplified.

Paej 21a (This paej iz in Baesik Inglish Maed Simpəl) (BI)

Numbers Simplified/Numberz Simplified 0-660 oi-archon

oi		0	zero	0	loo		88	55
ae		1	one	1	on	N	60	60
ee		٢	two	2	nar		66	66
ie		3	three	3	op	P	ə0	70
oe		ε	four	4	per		əə	77
oo		8	five	5	oɣə	¥	℮0	80
ar		6	six	6	ɣor		℮℮	88
er		ə	seven	7	oz	Z	90	90
or		℮	eight	8	zou		99	99
ou		9	nine	9	**och**	**CH**	**100**	**100**
ob	**B**	**10**	**ten**	**10**	chae		101	101
bae		11	eleven	11	chee		10٢	102
bee		1٢	twelve	12	choe		10ε	104
bie		13	thirteen	13	chob		110	110
boe		1ε	fourteen	14	chobae		111	111
boo		18	fifteen	15	choboo		118	115
bar		16	sixteen	16	chol		180	150
ber		1ə	seventeen	17	eech		٢00	200
bor		1℮	eighteen	18	eechogar		٢٢6	226
bou		19	nineteen	19	eechokoo		٢ε8	245
og	**G**	٢0	twenty	20	iech		300	300
gae		٢1	twentyone	21	iechou		309	309
goo		٢8	twenty-five	25	iechogoo		3٢8	325
gou		٢9	twentynine	29	oech		ε00	400
oj	**J**	30	thirty	30	oechog		ε٢0	420
jee		3٢	thirty-two	32	oechozou		ε99	499
joe		3ε	thirty-four	34	ooch		800	500
ok	**K**	ε0	forty	40	oochol		880	550
kie		ε3	forty-three	43	arch		600	600
ol	**L**	80	fifty	50	archon		660	660

Numbers Simplified/Numberz Simplified 699-33000

archozou		699	699	Six hundred and ninety nine.
erch		∂00	700	
erchopoo		∂∂8	775	
erchozar		∂96	796	
orch		℮00	800	Eight hundred.
orchol		℮80	850	
orchopie		℮∂3	873	Eight hundred and seventy three.
ouch		900	900	
ouchor		908	905	
ouchozou		999	999	
om (1x000)	**M**	**1000**	**1000**	**One thousand.**
omae		1001	1001	
omeechojoe		1Γ3Ɛ	1234	One thousand two hundred and thirty four.
omoochol		1880	1550	
omouchozie		1993	1993	
eem		Γ000	2000	Two thousand.
eemee		Γ00Γ	2002	
eemochogae		Γ1Γ1	2121	
eemoochokie		Γ8Ɛ3	2543	Two thousand five hundred and forty three.
eemarchol		Γ680	2650	
iem		3000	3000	
iemiechozar		3396	3396	
oemoochonoo		Ɛ868	4565	Four thousand, five hundred and sixty five.
oomeechojoe		8Γ3Ɛ	5234	
armooch		6800	6500	
erm		∂000	7000	Seven thousand.
ormchogie		℮1Γ3	8123	
oumorchopar		9℮∂6	9876	Nine thousand, eight hundred & seventy six.
obomae		10001	10001	
ogiemoecholar		Γ3Ɛ86	23456	
ojiem		33000	33000	Thirty three thousand.

Numbers Simplified/Numberz Simplified 88/55,000 up

oloom/loom*		88 000	55 000
noom* oechojee		68 Ɛ3Ɩ	65 432
zoom		98 000	95 000
chom		100 000	100 000
chogiem oecholar		1Ɩ3 Ɛ86	123 456
iechokaem		3Ɛ1 000	341 000
oochom		800 000	500 000
archoporm ouchoɣer		6ə9 9əə	678 987
ercholom		ə80 000	750 000
orchogom		9Ɩ0 000	820 000
ouchobeem iechokoo		91Ɩ 3Ɛ8	912 345
od / one million (2x000)	**D**	**1 000 000**	**1 000 000**
eed		Ɩ 000 000	2 000 000
ied oochonerm		3 86ə 000	3 567 000
oedob		Ɛ 000 010	4 000 010
oodoocholoom oochol		8 888 880	5 555 550
ardochogiem oecholar		6 1Ɩ3 56Ɛ	6 123 456
erdorchozor erchonoo		ə 69ə 68ə	7 898 765
ord		9 000 000	8 000 000
ordarcholom		9 680 000	8 650 000
oudouchozoum ouchozou		9 999 999	9 999 999
obod/bod*		10 000 000	10 000 000

olied archozom		83 690 000	53 690 000
ochozood		198 000 000	195 000 000
archoɣod		6ə0 000 000	680 000 000
ot / one billion (3x000)	**(T)**	**1 000 000 000**	**1 000 000 000**
teechojoed oochonerm orchoz			1 234 567 890
1 Ɩ3Ɛ 86ə ə90			
ietoecholard		3 Ɛ86 000 000	3 456 000 000

(*oloom/loom: front 'o' can be dropped if not needed)

three billion, four hundred and fifty six million.

Numbers Simplified/Numberz Simplified   Up to 10^{30} (osh)

artiecholod	6 380 000 000	6 350 000 000
ozot	90 000 000 000	90 000 000 000
of / one trillion **F (4** x 000)		1 000 000 000 000
oqə / one quadrillion **Q (5** x 000)		1 000 000 000 000 000
os / one quintillion **S (6)**		1 000 000 000 000 000 000
ov / one sextillion **V (7)**		1 000 000 000 000 000 000 000
ost / septillion **ST (8)**		1 000 000 000 000 000 000 000 000
olk / octillion **LK (9)**		1 000 000 000 000 000 000 000 000 000
osh / nonillion **(10) SH**		1 000 000 000 000 000 000 000 000 000 000

The above is admittedly very simplified to quickly get through to the high numbers. We will backtrack now in smaller script to include the new digits and more random numbers, including a few long-winded English numbers to make a point. (It is noted that Americans do miss out some of the 'and's.)

123 456…   *one hundred and twenty three thousand, four hundred and fifty six.*

1ˇ3 ℰ86…chogiem oecholar.   **M 10^3**

9 876 543 ….. *nine million, eight hundred and seventy six, five hundred and forty three.*

9 eə6 8ℰ3 … oudorchopar oochokie.   **D 10^6**

53 690 000.. *fifty three million, six hundred and ninety thousand.*

83 690 000… olied archozom.

576 923 225…. *five hundred and seventy six million, nine hundred and twenty*

8ə6 9ˇ3 ˇˇ8.. oochopard ouchogiem eechogoo. *three thousand,two hundred and twenty five.*

3 560 000 000.. *three billion, five hundred and sixty million.*

3 860 000 000.. ietoochonod.   **T 10^9**

6 230 500 000 000….. *six trillion, two hundred and thirty billion, five hundred*

6 ˇ30 800 000 000..arfeechojot oochod.   **F 10^{12}** *million.*

1 236 459 000 000 000 …..*one quadrillion, two hundred and thirty six trillion, four hundred and fifty nine billion.*

1 ˇ36 ℰ89 000 000 000.. qeechojarf oecholoud.   **Q 10^{15}**

2 000 000 000 000 000 000…*two quintillion*

ˇ 000 000 000 000 000 000…ees.   **S 10^{18}**

3 000 000 000 000 000 000 000…*three sextillion.*   **V 10^{21}…iev**

4 000 000 000 000 000 000 000 000.. *four septillion.*

ℰ 000 000 000 000 000 000 000 000..oest.   **st 10^{24}**

5 x 10^{27}..*five octillion.* **8 x 10^{27}..oolk.**   **lk 10^{27}**

9 x 10^{30}..*nine nonillion.* **9 x 10^{30}..oush.**   **sh 10^{30}**

Picking the Consonants for Numbers Simplified

Note that **NS is complete and workable the way it is.** What we do with it next is largely up to others. Those interested, perhaps in the category of mathematicians or scientists mentioned in the last paragraph of page 21, feel free to contact the author. Also, it would be good to finish with a **very simple chart**, to show how simple and understandable this subject is, along with a few notes.

(Note: trad Eng number symbols on this page (1, 2, 3, 4, 5); NS symbols over)

1 ae You will see the logic in picking these hard vowels, **alphabetical as 1-5,** and then
2 ee again as **6-9**. Nine **(ou)** and zero **(oi)** were picked last; as in traditional English, **oi**
3 ie is not used to describe a number total.
4 oe
5 oo
6 ar (**ar/er/or** work well as vowels, but cancel out using the 'r' as a consonant)
7 er
8 or
9 ou (avoid 'w' as 'ow' but can use 'okwə' in the '-illions')
10 b Consonant sounds have been chosen for better differentiation and to follow
20 g the alphabet, as noted at the bottom of page 20.
30 j
40 k There is nothing to forbid putting 'ae' (one) in front of 'ch', 'm', 'd', etc.
50 l It is like saying '**one** hundred/thousand' instead of '**a** hundred/thousand'.
60 n (och/aech, om/aem, od/aed) Don't try it with tens/twenties, however.
70 p
80 ɣ (oɣə uses 'ɣ' (yae); don't confuse with vowel sounds 'oi/oy')
90 z
100 och (take 'c' for century out of 'ch' to remember this one)
1 000 (1) om (as explained on p 21, 'mille' is a thousand)
1 000 000 (2) od (2 x 000)
1 000 000 000 (3) ot
1 000 000 000 000 (4) of ('ov' and 'of' are close sounds, however)
1 000 000 000 000 000 (5) oqə (okwə in BI)
1 000 000 000 000 000 000 (6) os
1 000 000 000 000 000 000 000 (7) ov (the 'v' in seven might help to remember)
1 000 000 000 000 000 000 000 000 (8) ost (s and k are used a lot, as options run out)
1 000 000 000 000 000 000 000 000 000 (9) olk (can reverse: **kloochost** 1500+000x8)
1 000 000 000 000 000 000 000 000 000 000 (10) osh

Piking thə Konsənəntz for Numberz Simplified

Noet that **NS iz kompléet and werkəbəl thə way it iz.** Wot wee doo with it next iz larjly up too utherz. Thoez intrəstəd, perhápz in thə katigəry ov maphəmatíshənz or sieəntistz menshənd in thə lâst pa'rəgrâf ov paej 21, feel free too kontakt thee aupher. Aulsoe, it wəd bee gəd too finish with ə **ve'ry simpəl chart**, too shoe how simpəl and understándəbəl this subjekt iz.

(Noet: NS (1,Γ,3,Ɛ,8) and trad Eng number simbəlz on this paej)

1 ae

Γ ee (2)

3 ie

Ɛ oe (4)

8 oo (5)

6 ar

ə er (7)

ℓ or (8)

9 ou

10 b

Γ0 g (20)

30 j

Ɛ0 k (40)

80 l (50)

60 n

ə0 p (70)

ℓ0 ɣ (80)

90 z

100 och

1 000 (1) om

1 000 000 (2) ob (Γx000)

1 000 000 000 (3) ot

1 000 000 000 000 (4) of (Ɛx000)

1 000 000 000 000 000 (5) oqə (8x000)

1 000 000 000 000 000 000 (6) os

1 000 000 000 000 000 000 000 (7) ov (əx000)

1 000 000 000 000 000 000 000 000 (8) ost (ℓx000)

1 000 000 000 000 000 000 000 000 000 (9) osk

1 000 000 000 000 000 000 000 000 000 000 (10) osh

Paej 24a (This paej iz in Advâncd Inglish Maed Simpəl) (AI)

About the Author

Born in southern England, right after World War II. An interesting childhood in Kampala, Uganda and the Usambara Mountains of Tanganyika. Three eventful sea trips back to the UK, through the Suez and around the Cape of Good Hope. Returns to Entebbe across the Sahara in small airport-hopping planes. Prep school in the jungle, Public school in Berkshire, England. As site engineer/surveyor, Chris works and attends college in England. Moonlighting weekends with an ice cream van helps get him to New York. New life in the New World at 23, exploring the United States for six months in the hippy seventies, followed by a dash of Mexico, and immigration to Canada. Driven more by Geography than by career, Chris mixes survey work in Manitoba and the Yukon, with lumberjacking BC and roughnecking Alberta. Embracing near Arctic winters on snow-shoe surveys and frozen tundra drilling, he intersperses his time in Ottawa, Toronto and Vancouver with volunteer administration work, philosophical studies, and weekend taxi driving. A three month trip through the Maritimes as advanced PR for police reform, leaves only Newfoundland unvisited, and the moniker 'travelling limey' starts to take shape.

After Canadian citizenship, a trip to southern California becomes semi-permanent, dividing time between theology studies and selling goods on the roadside. From laser pictures displayed on empty Hollywood lots, the one-man mobile business expands across southern California and jumps to the east coast and Florida, as the spirit demands. In 1984, yours truly makes his first circle of the globe, including an overland trip from London to Kathmandu. Descending into New Delhi from the Himalayas, he runs into a three day riot of fires and burning buses, following the assassination of Indira Ghandi, as he and the bus driver escape from a series of fiery ambushes. Back in the USA, a cabin in the San Bernardino mountains has become this lifetime's main home and anchor, joined by a wife for too short a time. The main roadside products are now rugs and flags, with bobbydazzling displays the size of a medium parking lot. Dividing time between California and Florida, greener pastures are found near the beautiful Sierra mountains, northern Nevada, Utah and Wyoming on the west; North Carolina and Massachusetts on the east. In the end, Wisconsin, the Arctic islands and Labrador are the only areas of this amazing continent not yet explored. Back home in Vancouver, Canada since 2018.

The above is this time around. Before that, things were tied up with crazy wars on the European subcontinent and beyond. But the time before saw some good use of the English language, still enjoyed by many today.. The seeds of this book were planted then.

Page 25a (This is the last page of Inglish Maed Simpəl. Begin!)

Printed in the United States
By Bookmasters